THE ART OF

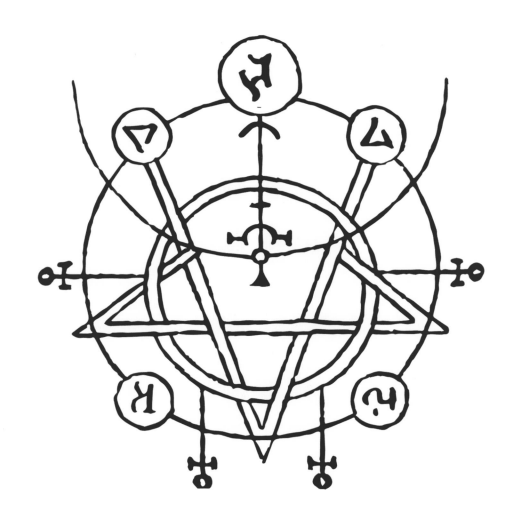

CONTENTS

FOREWORD

BY BROM

ometime around 1996, a curse was placed upon me. That curse came in the form of a PC game titled Diablo. Games had just been games up until then, but Diablo crept into my psyche and wouldn't leave. It got to the point (when my twenty-minute Diablo break far too often exceeded two hours)

where I had to have my wife hide the playing disk so that I could get my actual work done.

So imagine my utter joy and astonishment when, out of the blue, I got a call from Blizzard inviting me to paint the cover for *Diablo II*. I responded with a resounding, "Yes! Why, yes, I would!" Creating art for something I thoroughly love, like *Diablo*, is illustration at its finest. For me, it is akin to fine art.

And *Diablo*, in all its forms, has always been more than a game. It's a mood, an experience—visually and viscerally—thanks to the way the intensity of gameplay burns the sounds and images into your consciousness. Even now, I can close my eyes and see, hear, and feel the brutal grunts of the Butcher and the infernal bleating of those demon goat beasts. *Diablo* conjures an instantly recognizable, immersive nightmarish dreamscape like no other game before or after.

There has always been an edge to *Diablo*, one I equate with the taste of cold steel. The

challenge for me as an illustrator is to try and capture that edge, that intensity, that wickedness. Luckily, I have had a lot of help throughout the years from the *Diablo* team and its unmatched character designers, who bring me reams of brilliant art, giving me the opportunity to plunder their designs, to interpret them, and to mesh together the work into my own aesthetic. It's collaboration at its finest and one of the most creatively satisfying experiences of my career.

Working with such high-level talent, you can't fake it. You have to do your best; otherwise, you might let the team down. There's a rush of adrenaline and excitement that comes from working with such motivated and accomplished people that pushes you to excel, and as a result, I feel I painted some of my top personal work in the genre while working on *Diablo*.

Thank you, Team *Diablo*. Thank you for inviting me to play in your wicked and epic sandbox!

"The original painting has a big hole in his head. That was how it was going to go on the box, but Columbine happened and Blizzard became nervous that it would be associated with the shooting, like there's a bullet hole in his head. So when you see the final cover, the hood has been lowered and that hole has been covered up."

—BROM

INTRODUCTION

BY CHRIS METZEN

Nineteen ninety-six feels like such a long time ago. Warcraft II had just hit. We'd just announced StarCraft. And then a whole bunch of us down in Irvine got our hands on the project from the crew up north. It was code-named "Condor," and when I first heard about it, it was a turn-based RPG set in a fantasy world. But by the time those of us in the south finally got to sculpt some story for it, it had changed a lot.

It was real-time. It was dark. It was gory.

It was *Diablo*.

Screenshots don't do the memories justice. It was so different from what we had been doing at the time. And there were all these technical things that pushed it into a class of its own. The way you couldn't see around corners, the way there was just a little pool of light around your character that made the rest of the level fall away into shadows (a huge achievement back then), the way demons would just charge at you . . .

Oh yeah, the demons. The setting. I was in love.

A sword-swinging boss with a crown on his head called the Skeleton King? The Sin War? The big red dude waiting for you in the depths of hell?

There was a lot of inspiring stuff to work with. If you look at my old art in the *Diablo* manual, you'll see I started drawing on blacked-out paper, just to make sure it all looked dark enough. I loved the way that game felt.

And then Blizzard North sent it into the stratosphere. They took the series out of a single town and into the huge, strange world of Sanctuary, where we got to make some of the most unique stuff Blizzard ever shipped, in my opinion.

When *Diablo* fired on all cylinders, there was nothing else like it, and the way it felt had so much to do with the way it looked.

I'm glad I got to spend some time in Tristram, in Kehjistan, in the Burning Hells, and in the High Heavens.

The next time I go back will be as a player, just like all of you. I can't wait.

OPPOSITE The Corruption of Prince Albrecht + *Diablo* Game Manual + Chris Metzen

ABOVE Demon + *Diablo* Game Manual + Samwise Didier

FOLLOWING PAGES *Diablo III* PvP Banner + *Diablo III* + Laurel Austin

"When I was drawing images for the *Diablo* manual, I started drawing everything on a full-black background to match how dark and disturbing the game felt to me. . . . I wanted to create a tragic, mythological feeling for the origin of this entire world."

—CHRIS METZEN, former Senior Vice President of Story and Franchise Development

The Diablo series of games will be remembered for many things: for exemplifying the action RPG genre, for offering exhilarating co-op play, and for serving up punishing procedural dungeons that are always full of surprises. But what is arguably Diablo's most enduring contribution to the genre is its unforgettable dark tone.

The *Diablo* games tell tales of reluctant mortals caught in the middle of the Eternal Conflict, forced to protect the earthly realm of Sanctuary against both the evils of the Burning Hells and the angels of the High Heavens.

The darkness of *Diablo* comes through in the brutal gameplay, as heroes find themselves swarmed by deadly enemies, hanging on by a thread, desperately trying to defeat unspeakable monsters before their lifeblood spills to the thirsty ground beneath their feet.

By equal measure, the darkness and horror of the world are delivered via the visual experience of *Diablo*. One can look at a screenshot of a *Diablo* game and know without a doubt where it comes from. *Diablo* has its own brand of darkness—one that millions of fans around the world yearn to embrace. "For everything in *Diablo*, we painted

with a darker brush, literally and figuratively," comments Senior Art Director Samwise Didier.

How the artists at Blizzard Entertainment create that feeling through strong, defining visual ideas is what this book is about. There is a carefully crafted art to the horrific dread that *Diablo* inspires, which has made it such a defining experience for its loyal legion of fans.

Among those fans are current creators, including *Diablo IV* Art Director John Mueller, who was inspired by *Diablo II*, released in 2000. "It was a really impactful game," he recalls. "It's one of those things that has stood the test of time. The thing that I remember was just how frightening the world was."

Looking back at *Diablo* and *Diablo II* decades later, it's hard to understand how small, pixelated forms inspired so much dread. Part of the

answer lies with the vivid artwork that shipped with the games in their manuals. "With *Diablo* and *Diablo II*, there was no real art done for that game, in terms of concepts," recalls Didier. "The main artwork that everyone associated with it was from the manual. We were working on the game, and then when the game was done, we had to put together a manual, and that's when we did art that would help sell what the game was supposed to look like in your mind."

Fast-forward almost twenty years, and video game design has evolved dramatically. Art is on the front end of the development process as a defining conceptual practice rather than being a post-production activity that fills in the picture. Today, the *Diablo* art team works relentlessly to define what all aspects of the game will look like, making sure

that every character, creature, item, and environment cleaves to the game's guiding aesthetics.

Mueller places *Diablo*'s Gothic visual signature—and its capacity to frighten—in the tradition of dark fantasy spawned by the folklore of medieval Europe. "I think of *Diablo* like it's classic European folklore, as opposed to Tolkien fantasy," he says. "In Tolkien fantasy, there're all these races and there's a world that is not our world. European folklore tends to be a lot more about us. It's more about people. There are these things that torture us and things that hurt us and things in the dark and things that are frightening. I think that's where *Diablo* comes from.

"It's like the dark edges of your imagination. It's like people bring something to it that we can't anticipate because it's their own fear."

OPPOSITE Angel + *Diablo* Game Manual + Samwise Didier
ABOVE Demon Sky Concept + *Diablo III* + Victor Lee

Characters

Diablo character design is governed by two main principles. To begin, any character—whether a hero, a key non-player character, or a boss—must represent a signature take on a fantasy archetype such as a warrior, demon, or angel. Second, the character's design must tell a story. Both of these rules are especially important for the game's heroes, which are any player's main point of identification.

"Whenever we start to talk about a new class, we look at what the fantasy is and then ask ourselves, *How can we make it our own?*" says Art Director John Mueller. "There are some tropes that you've got to carry. Then you've got to figure out what your spin is that makes them iconic."

This principle of crafting recognizable-but-unique fantasy archetypes has been important to every *Diablo* game and even spans releases. The artists working on *Diablo III*, for example, had to strive to create new versions of elements that had become established as iconic in the *Diablo* universe itself, such as the Barbarian, the Khazra, the town of Tristram, and even Diablo himself.

Conveying backstory via design features is more than just a design principle for *Diablo* artists; it resonates with the world depicted in the games. For the immortals, such as the Great Evils and the members of the Angiris Council, the Eternal Conflict has raged for eons, making the past deeply present. And for the mortal humans, their lives are haunted by history and driven by a struggle to resist forces beyond their comprehension.

"In *Diablo,* there's no happiness," says Senior Art Director Samwise Didier. "Anyone who's a hero is a hero because he's *had* to fight. He's the last surviving member of his family, and he's worn, and tattered, and beat."

The Barbarian

The tribes in the north know the depths of Sanctuary's darkness all too well. Their purpose, handed down from their great ancestor Bul-Kathos, was to protect the secrets of Mount Arreat, the mountain that has cast a shadow across their culture for its entire existence. Their warriors are trained in hand-to-hand warfare from a young age and revel in the chance to test their might against worthy foes, forging their reputations in the blood of their vanquished enemies.

The Barbarian, born of this brutal tradition, debuted in *Diablo II* as a topknotted, tattooed warrior with an instinct for battle and a thirst for close-quarter melee. It would have been very easy for the Barbarian to have a lot of visual similarities to other fantasy brutes, but the team at Blizzard North worked hard to give him his own unique appearance.

"For me, Conan the Barbarian is the pinnacle, and I probably couldn't see past that," says Senior Art Director Sam Didier. "These guys were good enough to go, 'We could do something that's more Blizzard, more our own.'"

Twenty years later in-game, at the start of *Diablo III*, the homeland of the Barbarian tribes around Mount Arreat has been reduced to rubble and isolated fortifications. The longevity of the barbarians' fight and their world-weariness is reflected in the age of the male version of their champion—a gray-bearded veteran who can't quit killing demons and acquiring scars.

The "Barb," as the old veteran became known among the artists, is flanked by a flame-haired female Barbarian, a younger brawler with a penchant for axes and blue war paint. Every bit as tough as her male counterpart, she is hungry to make her mark on the battlefield. "I wanted her to look like she could do all the things the Barb can do," says Senior Artist Phroilan Gardner. "So I wasn't going to make her yet another slender female warrior. This girl was going be physically imposing. I feel like that approach is underused in fantasy and made for a more memorable fem-barb."

BELOW Male Barbarian Sketch ✦
Diablo III ✦ Duncan Fegredo

BOTTOM Male Barbarian Concept ✦
Diablo III ✦ Josh Tallman

RIGHT Medium Barbarian Study ✦
Diablo III ✦ Phroilan Gardner

OPPOSITE, TOP Barbarian Key Art
Study ✦ *Diablo III* ✦ Josh Tallman

OPPOSITE, BOTTOM Barbarian Key
Art ✦ *Diablo III* ✦ Josh Tallman

FOLLOWING PAGES Barbarian
Concept ✦ *Diablo III* ✦ Trent Kaniuga

The Crusader

ABOVE Crusader Rune + *Diablo III: Reaper of Souls* + Uncredited

BELOW Crusader Sketch + *Diablo III: Reaper of Souls* + Mark Gibbons

RIGHT Male Inquisitor Sketch + *Diablo III: Reaper of Souls* + Chris Ha

BOTTOM LEFT Crusader Concept + *Diablo III: Reaper of Souls* + Josh Tallman

BOTTOM RIGHT Dark Crusader Concept + *Diablo III: Reaper of Souls* + Victor Lee

OPPOSITE Female Crusader Concept + *Diablo III: Reaper of Souls* + Glenn Rane

All Crusaders swear an oath to dedicate their lives to exterminating the corruption within their faith. They abandon their names, their families, and their past deeds, searching the world for a way to restore the Zakarum Church to purity once again. Theirs is a lonely existence, each with only an apprentice to share the journey. And the day they fall, their apprentice will take up their shields and continue on with their cause.

The Paladin class in *Diablo II*—also a Zakarum warrior—had shown the glory of unleashing righteous power upon the armies of evil. In the *Diablo III* expansion *Reaper of Souls*, the Crusader was designed to fill a similar role as an ultraheavy holy champion. But the art team didn't want this brick of a hero to wield typical knightly weapons such as swords and maces. Instead, they opted for flails, which conjure images of religious flagellants who beat themselves to show their devotion.

"We thought about things like an executioner or some kind of very zealous religious knight," says Senior Concept Artist Josh Tallman. "It's like, 'Wait, hold on a second. A Crusader on a mission to destroy all demons?' That's not as nice-sounding as an 'uphold justice' knight."

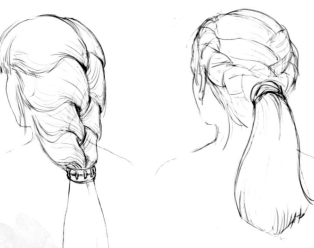

"The Crusader is a very zealous kind of knight. So it was based on the idea of a flagellant, who whips themselves, and we decided their signature weapon would be a flail. Not that they whip themselves with it, but it associates that kind of imagery with the design."

—JOSH TALLMAN, Senior Concept Artist

The Demon Hunter

ABOVE Demon Hunter Fan of Knives Rune + *Diablo III* + Uncredited

BELOW Demon Hunter Sketch + *Diablo III* + Richie Marella

RIGHT Demon Hunter Concept + *Diablo III* + Jeff Kang

BOTTOM Demon Hunter Concepts + *Diablo III* + Uncredited

OPPOSITE Demon Hunter + BlizzCon 2010 Key Art + Glenn Rane

I n Sanctuary, every hero who gazes into the darkness knows the risk of being consumed by it. But for the Demon Hunter, darkness is not a risk but a welcome certainty. Fueled by hatred and tempered by discipline, each lethal member of their order willingly accepts any price to claim his or her deepest desire: vengeance.

Early game designs for *Diablo III* called for a ranged hero—agile and able to damage enemies from a distance. The art team initially developed concepts for a desert ranger, someone who roamed the northern wastelands before making the journey to New Tristram. But the class needed something—a motivation, a touch of darkness—to place it properly in the *Diablo* universe. Enter the Demon Hunter, who has a favored enemy ingrained in their psyche, courtesy of a deep childhood trauma.

Earlier versions of the Demon Hunter's backstory imagined the class as half-demonic, capable of manifesting hellish powers and shape changing into a creature of the Burning Hells. Ultimately, the crossbreed idea was rejected. The citizens of Sanctuary could never accept such a being. The dark side of the Demon Hunter became more psychological and aesthetic, with the final "evil Robin Hood" look taking hold—complete with its cowl, scarf, crossbows, and formfitting armor.

OPPOSITE, TOP LEFT Naked Ranger Study + *Diablo III* + Phroilan Gardner

OPPOSITE, TOP MIDDLE Heavy Ranger Study + *Diablo III* + Josh Tallman

OPPOSITE, TOP RIGHT Medium Ranger Study + *Diablo III* + Josh Tallman

OPPOSITE, BOTTOM LEFT & BOTTOM RIGHT Ranger Concepts + *Diablo III* + Josh Tallman

ABOVE Work-in-Progress Demon Hunter Concept + *Diablo III* + Victor Lee

FAR LEFT Demon Huntress Concept + *Diablo III* + Richie Marella

LEFT Bone Huntress Concept + *Diablo III* + Victor Lee

"Game Design wanted a ranged archer who was very fast and mobile and used crossbows or bows. One of the designs the team really liked was Phroilan Gardner's take on it, which was a desert ranger. I wouldn't say that the ranger evolved into the Demon Hunter; it was more like, 'Let's do a ranger.' And then, for some reason, 'OK, let's try something else.' And the Demon Hunter is what came out of that."

—JOSH TALLMAN, Senior Concept Artist

The Monk

ABOVE Monk Class Crest +
Diablo III + Trent Kaniuga

BELOW Monk Arm Study +
Diablo III + Josh Tallman

RIGHT Monk Sketch + *Diablo III* +
Josh Tallman

MIDDLE RIGHT Monk Portrait +
Diablo III + Josh Tallman

BOTTOM LEFT Heavy Monk Sketch +
Diablo III + Josh Tallman +

BOTTOM MIDDLE & BOTTOM RIGHT
Medium Monk Concepts + *Diablo III* +
Josh Tallman

OPPOSITE Monk Concept + *Diablo III* +
Phroilan Gardner

I n a world beset by corruption, a pure spirit contains immense potential. The devout initiates of the Sahptev faith spend years training themselves to overcome and eradicate their flaws, and the results are calm, measured warriors capable of unleashing the will of their gods upon any unfortunate creatures who confront them.

The Monk presented a unique challenge to the *Diablo III* artists: How would they make a melee class that doesn't wear armor and uses only the simplest weapons appear robust enough to face hordes of beasts, demons, and undead on the front line? "One of the ideas was for the armor to be giant on the arms," recalls Senior Concept Artist Josh Tallman. "His body would still be mostly cloth or still compact, but the arms would have giant armor."

Under the bulky armor, the orange robes of Shaolin monks provided an obvious point of inspiration, but the *Diablo* team wanted to give their Monk a unique cultural twist. Locating the order in Ivgorod, they crossed Russian Orthodox Christian monks' Caucasian facial features and long beards with East Asian monks' saffron vestments, leg wraps, and shaved heads to create a new breed of Monk.

RIGHT Male Monk Lineup + *Diablo III* +
Josh Tallman

BELOW Monk Concept + *Diablo III* +
Josh Tallman

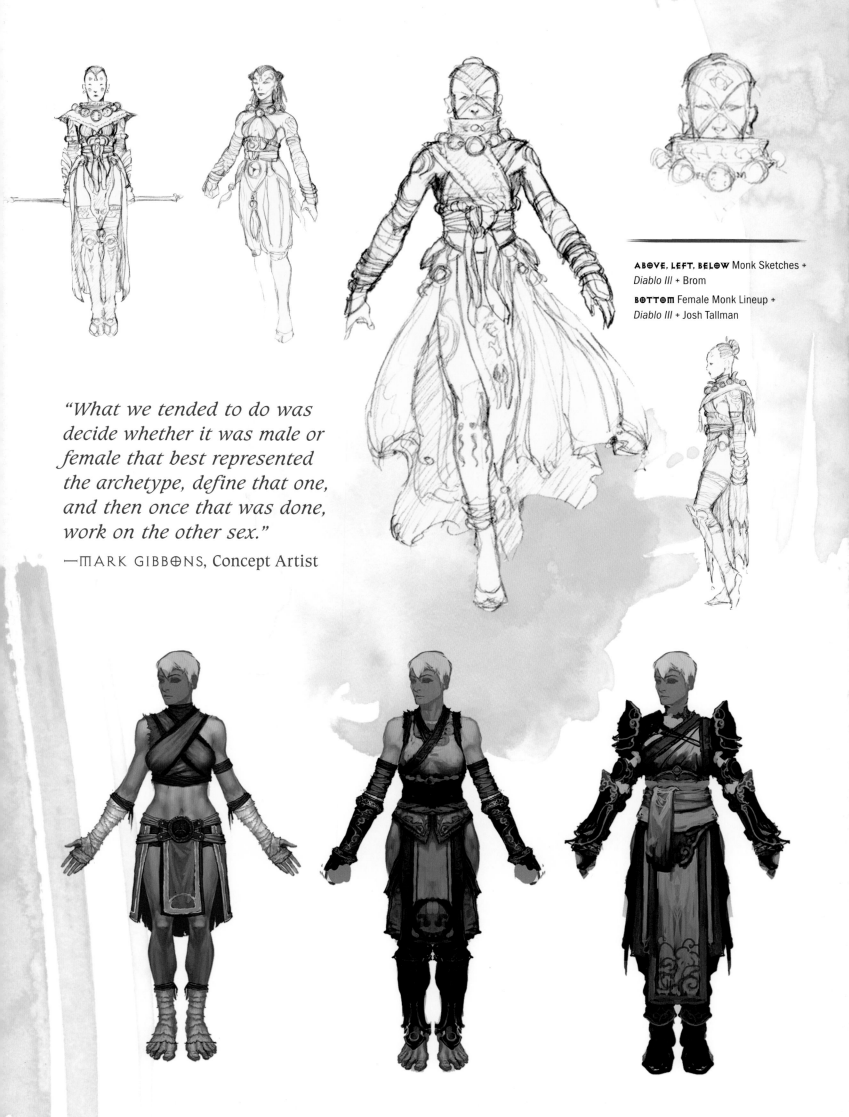

ABOVE, LEFT, BELOW Monk Sketches ✦ *Diablo III* ✦ Brom

BOTTOM Female Monk Lineup ✦ *Diablo III* ✦ Josh Tallman

"What we tended to do was decide whether it was male or female that best represented the archetype, define that one, and then once that was done, work on the other sex."

—MARK GIBBONS, Concept Artist

41

OPPOSITE Monk + *Diablo III* + Brom

LEFT Female Monk Concept + *Diablo III* +Josh Tallman

BELOW Female Monk Portrait + *Diablo III* + Josh Tallman

BOTTOM Heavy Monk Study + *Diablo III* +Josh Tallman

FOLLOWING PAGES Monk Key Art + *Diablo III* + Josh Tallman

The Necromancer

Even among those who wield the supernatural, the forces of death are taboo. They believe that tampering with the souls and flesh of the departed must certainly be a sin, a defilement, an unclean act. But to the Necromancer, the horrors of death are a symphony of possibilities. Every corpse is a weapon, every bone is a piece of armor, and every soul is a soldier. The course of life leads inexorably to death, and it should not be feared. Instead, the cycle should be protected at all costs.

In some ways, the Necromancer was the star of *Diablo II*. It was rare to see such dark, evil-looking magic in the hands of a game protagonist. That headlining stature never left the class, which got a dedicated content pack for *Diablo III* called *Rise of the Necromancer*. "We were trying to come up with our idea of what was going to be cool about the *Diablo III* version of the Necromancer," recalls Art Director John Mueller. "We came upon the theme of 'rock star.' Basically, they have very big, over-the-top effects. We realized that this is a performer, that this is somebody who has an entourage. There were a lot of cool associations that we could make with that vibe."

True to celebrity form, the Necromancer makes his or her red-carpet appearances only in the most fashionable attire, including armor made out of human skin and working organs that splash blood on the ground, courtesy of the visual effects team.

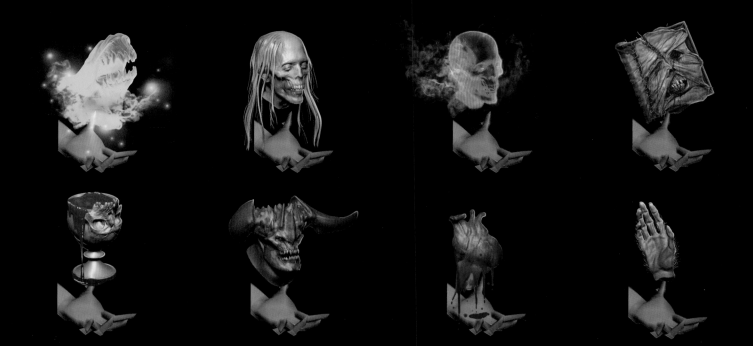

ABOVE Necromancer 3D Models ✦ *Diablo III: Rise of the Necromancer* ✦ Chris Amaral

BELOW Marketing Panel Art ✦ *Diablo III: Rise of the Necromancer* ✦ Josh Tallman

OPPOSITE, TOP Necromancer Skeleton Concepts ✦ *Diablo III: Rise of the Necromancer* ✦ Chris Amaral

OPPOSITE, BOTTOM BlizzCon 2016 Announcement Art ✦ *Diablo III: Rise of the Necromancer* ✦ John Mueller

"Rise of the Necromancer *was an opportunity to reimagine a classic class in the style of* Diablo III. *It's also one of the most beloved classes, I think, because you get to play a monster, essentially. And people really love being dark and evil.*"

—JOHN MUELLER, Art Director

The Witch Doctor

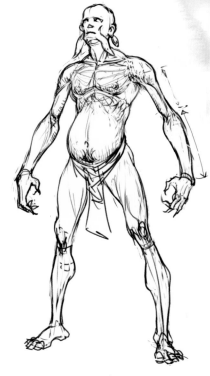

ew are blessed with the ability to commune with spirits who have passed on, and very few of those have the courage to seek their aid. The Witch Doctors from the eastern lands of Sanctuary wield their gifts with care and precision, assaulting their enemies with curses, poisons, and the fury of countless lost spirits.

The Witch Doctor works his or her magic by putting together visceral arrangements of discarded, forgotten things—found objects, organic material gone to rot, and skulls and other bones. *Diablo III*'s oddball hero from the start, the Witch Doctor is a playable class as pastiche, recasting elements of the Druid and Necromancer from *Diablo II* while adding that game's troublesome Fetishes to its army of pets. Combining disturbing companions, riotous colors, over-the-top masks, and bizarre spell effects, the Witch Doctor gave the *Diablo* artists a chance to explore an entirely new form of dark magic. "It was like, well, what's the craziest thing we could come up with?" recounts Senior Art Supervisor Justin Thavirat. "The exploding creatures and the falling zombie walls, and things like that, are pretty rad."

OPPOSITE, TOP LEFT Witch Doctor
Concept + *Diablo III* + Duncan Fegredo

OPPOSITE, TOP RIGHT Horrify Spell
Concept + *Diablo III* + Josh Tallman

OPPOSITE, BOTTOM Wall of Zombies
Spell Concept + *Diablo III* + Josh Tallman

ABOVE LEFT Female Witch Doctor
Silhouettes + *Diablo III* + Josh Tallman

ABOVE Female Witch Doctor Sketch +
Diablo III + Cheeming Boey

LEFT Female Witch Doctor
Studies + *Diablo III* + Victor Lee

BELOW Witch Doctor Concept +
Diablo III + Victor Lee

PAGE 54 Witch Doctor +
Diablo III + Brom

PAGE 55 Female Witch Doctor
Concept + *Diablo III* + Glenn Rane

The Wizard

Superstition runs deep among the populace of Sanctuary. But perhaps that is for the best—for here, superstition is often rooted in truth. Every mage must ply their trade carefully for their own safety so as not to tread on the fears of the common folk, and most clans are averse to drawing attention to themselves.

The Sorceress who traveled to the Tamoe Mountains in *Diablo II* and the Wizard who followed a falling star to New Tristram in *Diablo III* are not like most mages. When evil rose, they boldly strode to meet it, using their unique powers to immolate everything in their path.

To come up with an original take on the fantasy mage archetype, the *Diablo III* art team not only had to contend with the hundreds of variations found in other games, but also needed to factor in the legacy of *Diablo*'s Sorcerer and *Diablo II*'s Sorceress. The Sorcerer exhibited Indian features, and the Sorceress appeared Egyptian, which made the *Diablo III* artists wonder if their Wizard could have another non-Western culture as a point of reference. They chose to make the character from Xiansai, *Diablo*'s equivalent of a Far Eastern nation.

To distinguish their Wizard's gameplay from past examples of a casting class, the artists decided to focus on making the spells visceral experiences, perhaps best exemplified by the hero's signature Disintegrate, a sustained beam of lethal power that blasts through enemies and can instantly cross the length of the player's view. "She almost feels like a sci-fi, missile-launching, laser beam–firing character," comments Senior Art Supervisor Justin Thavirat.

RIGHT Mage Sketch + *Diablo III* + Victor Lee

BOTTOM LEFT Wizard Sketch + *Diablo III* + Mark Gibbons

BOTTOM RIGHT Female Mage Sketch + *Diablo III* + Victor Lee

OPPOSITE Female Wizard Concept + *Diablo III* + Wei Wang

FOLLOWING PAGES Wizard Key Art + *Diablo III* + Josh Tallman

"We developed a feel for a rebellious, antiestablishment, nonstudious magic user. In some of the sketches, she's wearing a wizard's robe, but she's torn it down the middle and latched it back together. It's a hint of magical heritage that she's being sort of dismissive of."

—MARK GIBBONS, Concept Artist

Deckard Cain

"Stay awhile and listen."

When players first met Deckard Cain in *Diablo*, he was only a few pixels high. That form stayed constant in *Diablo II* but changed fundamentally in *Diablo III*, where he took on a short-lived but more intimate role, requiring a stronger visual presence. While Cain retained the white beard that goes with the territory for magic-wielding wise men, the *Diablo* art team put more of an emphasis on his piercing eyes and worn clothing, both of which speak to his long journey in search of knowledge.

And in keeping with the tone of the world, knowledge does not always bring peace. Deckard Cain spent decades burdened with terrible, terrible truths while always being driven to find more. His greatest gift is his greatest tragedy, for despite knowing that the end of days is nigh, he is powerless to stop it himself.

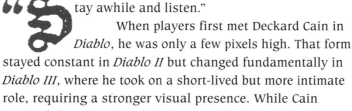

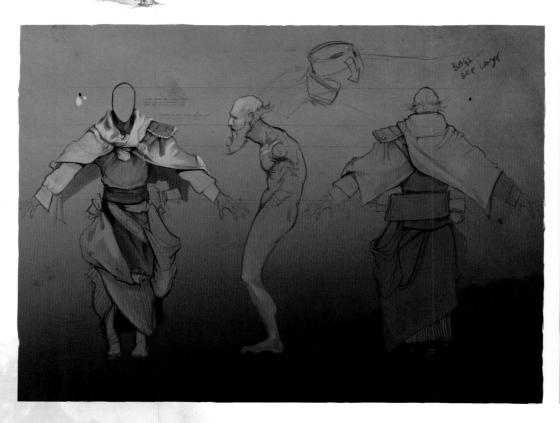

66

"Months before Diablo *was ever released, there was a contest to name an NPC. And this kid submitted his own name, 'Deckard Cain Elder.' And Bill Roper held that one up. 'Deckard Cain . . . the Elder. Doesn't that sound like a village wise man?' And so we built a character out of that."*

—CHRIS METZEN, former Senior Vice President
of Story and Franchise Development

Leah

70

ABOVE Prime Evil Throne Sketch +
Diablo III + Uncredited

RIGHT Leah Sketch + *Diablo III* +
Uncredited

BOTTOM Leah Orthographic Study +
Diablo III Cinematics + Brian Huang

OPPOSITE Leah Concept + *Diablo III*
Cinematics + Brian Huang

The Lords of Hell rarely roam Sanctuary in their true form. In *Diablo*, the Lord of Terror inhabited Albrecht, the youngest son of the mad king Leoric. In *Diablo II*, the Great Evil possessed the mind of the Dark Wanderer, the hero who defeated him. And in the third game, Diablo was reborn, not in the flesh of a child or a hero but as an innocent young woman named Leah, who was unknowingly created to be his vessel. It is she who aids the heroes who struggle to prevent the end of days, and it is she whom those heroes must destroy to stop Diablo.

Leah's lack of knowledge about her demonic heritage became an important part of the *Diablo III* story, underscored by her final young, spunky look and personality. But she wasn't always so innocent. When first thinking about Leah's design, Lead Concept Artist Victor Lee imagined her as a more worldly character—a precocious apprentice to her "Uncle Deckard." "The way I initially imagined Leah is somewhat of an older female," recalls Lee, "a bit less black and white, with some kind of pet demon. This Leah might dabble in some darker, unpermitted magic."

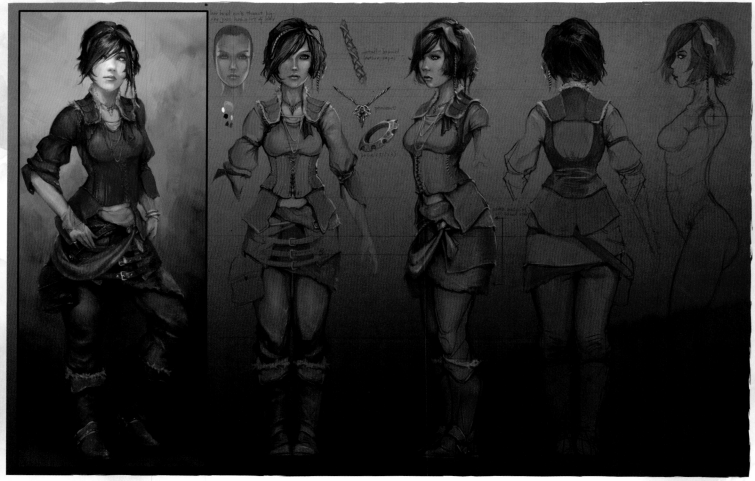

"This Leah might not know everything, but there's a certain courage to do questionable things. Almost like an adventurer kind of a character. She doesn't need to have her hand held all the time. She finds her own path."

—VICTOR LEE, Lead Concept Artist

RIGHT Leah Sketch + *Diablo III* + Victor Lee

BELOW Leah Portrait + *Diablo III* + Sojin Hwang

BOTTOM Leah Concept + *Diablo III* Cinematics + Brian Huang

OPPOSITE, TOP Leah, Drained + *Diablo III* Cinematics + Graven Tung

OPPOSITE, BOTTOM Surfacing Study + *Diablo III* Cinematics + Chris Thunig

Adria

A crucial conspirator in Diablo's secret plan to become the Prime Evil, Adria is the mother of Leah and a former member of the Coven. Having traveled throughout Sanctuary at the Lord of Terror's bidding and on her own quests for personal power, Adria is a mysterious nomad who possesses hidden knowledge.

A powerful witch who looks like a knowing Romani soothsayer, Adria holds deep secrets, which Lead Concept Artist Victor Lee suggested through body language and facial expressions. "She doesn't have any huge tomes or any scrolls or anything," he says. "I tried to ride the line between threatening and approachable because she's so mysterious. 'Is this a character to be feared or trusted? Which side do I nudge it?' I was constantly thinking about that."

Lee stresses that this level of consideration is crucial to good character design, even if the final avatar appears small on screen. The nuanced details of body language and facial expression in concept art become important tools for communicating with other departments responsible for bringing the characters to life, making the character more believable and coherent. "I always have this belief that designing a character is not just designing the costuming," he says. "I feel like you have to convey some of the beliefs and the characteristics of the person. That has to come across in the drawing."

BELOW Adria Demon Concepts +
Diablo III + Victor Lee

BOTTOM Adria Final Form Sketches +
Diablo III + Victor Lee

OPPOSITE Adria Concept +
Diablo III + Victor Lee

"Very little is known about Adria. She's almost nomad-like. I pulled a lot of the vibe of this character from Romani costumes, maybe a bit of belly-dancer ornamentation."
—VICTOR LEE, Lead Concept Artist

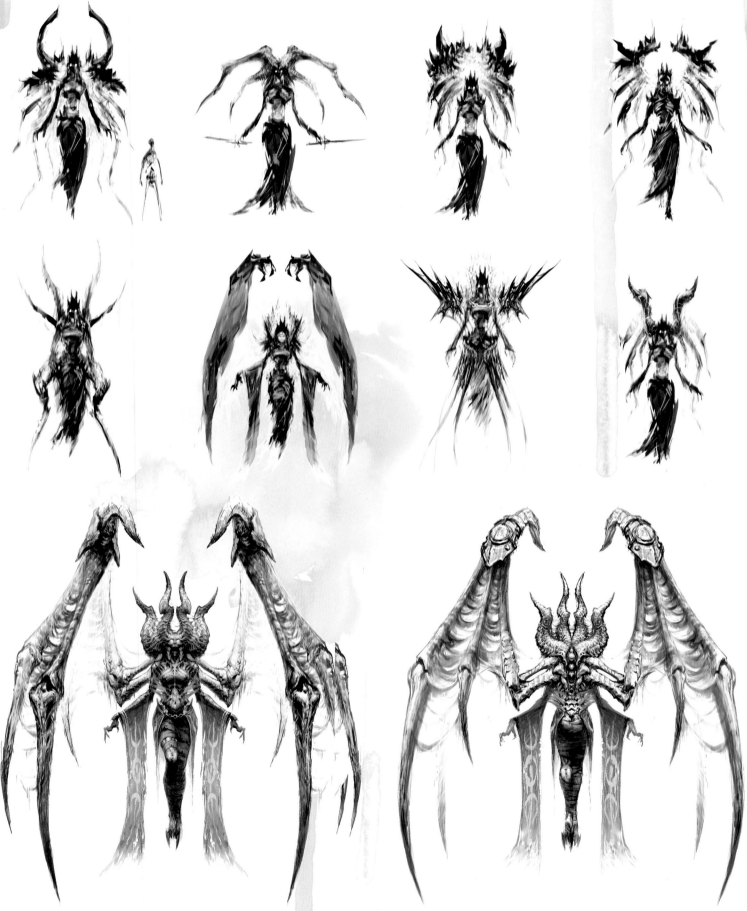

Followers

EIRENA, KORMAC & LYNDON

The three followers in *Diablo III*—Eirena the Enchantress, Kormac the Templar, and Lyndon the Scoundrel—are unique, capable characters with combat abilities that can complement any hero and distinctive designs meant to show the range of personalities that reside in Sanctuary. "The idea behind the followers was kind of like a miniature cast of the main archetypes," says Senior Concept Artist Josh Tallman. "You have the physical dude, you have the caster, and you have the ranged fighter."

With a certain overlap in roles between the followers and the heroes, the *Diablo III* artists had to be careful to make the henchmen distinct. They differentiated the supporting cast by creating simple designs that remained consistent throughout the game. "They have really one kind of costume that goes through light, medium, heavy," explains Tallman. "The costume doesn't change from, like, medieval armor to Aztec-themed armor to whatever. It just gets more elaborate."

OPPOSITE Templar Medium Study + *Diablo III* + Josh Tallman

ABOVE Stein Sigil + *Diablo III* + Banner Icon

BOTTOM LEFT Follower Head Studies + *Diablo III* + Josh Tallman

BOTTOM CENTER Enchantress Concept + *Diablo III* + Josh Tallman

BOTTOM RIGHT Scoundrel Concept + *Diablo III* + Josh Tallman

Artisans

HAEDRIG, MYRIAM & SHEN

The playable heroes of *Diablo* are unique; they are capable of battling evil while wielding dark, dangerous powers. They are meant to be expressions of humanity's true potential—remarkable and a little frightening.

By contrast, the supporting characters have always felt more personable and welcoming. The artisans who help empower players on their journey in *Diablo III* are cut from this cloth. But unlike the other merchants in each town, they must stand out since they follow the player to different locations and a player must always be able to recognize them instantly.

"The drawings and the design for the carts and the tents have a slightly different feel to them. The beams are a little thicker, and it's a slightly different read from the rest of things," observes Lead Concept Artist Victor Lee. "The world of *Diablo* is very, very dangerous. It's very dark, and it's very serious. You shouldn't be able to trust anybody in that world. But you should be able to trust these townspeople. Not everybody has to be a bandit or a murderer."

Other Humans

For secondary non-player characters (NPCs) in the *Diablo* games, the emphasis has always been on making sure that they are instantly legible from the isometric perspective. Each time players return to town, they must be able to quickly find who they need to talk to in order to advance the story. The role of each NPC needs to be clear at a glance—the towns' guards, the clerics who can heal you, the refugees who are huddled together in a tavern. They may have limited roles in gameplay, but they are critical for making each location feel alive and lived-in. "It's just giving them really good, strong silhouettes, making sure that they are readable from the game camera," explains Concept Artist Mark Gibbons. "They have to read from that angle, so you kind of exaggerate certain things."

Secondary NPCs also need to have a strong relationship with their environments to a higher degree than the characters who have their own agendas and who appear in different zones throughout the games. "Ideally, you make a character specific to the environment as well," explains Gibbons. "If the environment is extreme, then you expect that anything that you encounter in that environment will match it. As the game moves on, the environments get more fantastic, more imaginative, and so do the characters."

OPPOSITE NPC Portraits ✦ *Diablo III* ✦ Sojin Hwang

ABOVE Tristram Thug Sketch ✦ *Diablo III* ✦ Victor Lee

MIDDLE ROW, LEFT TO RIGHT Guard Sketch ✦ *Diablo II* ✦ Michio Okamura | Greiz Sketch ✦ *Diablo II* ✦ Michio Okamura | Meshif Sketch ✦ *Diablo II* ✦ Michio Okamura | Lysander Sketch ✦ *Diablo II* ✦ Michio Okamura | Edric Sketch ✦ *Diablo III* ✦ Josh Tallman

BOTTOM ROW, LEFT TO RIGHT Jerhyn Sketch ✦ *Diablo II* ✦ Michio Okamura | Charsi Sketch ✦ *Diablo II* ✦ Michio Okamura | Elzix Sketch ✦ *Diablo II* ✦ Michio Okamura | Reynald Sketch ✦ *Diablo III* ✦ Josh Tallman | Kashya Sketch ✦ *Diablo II* ✦ Michio Okamura

ARMOR- HEAVILY
PADDED CLOTH &
STUDDED LEATHER.
ODD PIECES OF
PLATE MAIL.

RIGHT Tristram Militia Sketches +
Diablo III + Mark Gibbons

BOTTOM LEFT Gravedigger Sketch +
Diablo III + Mark Gibbons

BOTTOM RIGHT Grave Robber
Sketch + *Diablo III* + Mark Gibbons

OPPOSITE, TOP LEFT Caldeum Spear
Troop Sketch + *Diablo III* + Victor Lee

OPPOSITE, TOP CENTER Caldeum Officer
Sketch + *Diablo III* + Victor Lee

OPPOSITE, TOP RIGHT Caldeum Cleaver
Troop Sketch + *Diablo III* + Victor Lee

OPPOSITE, BOTTOM LEFT Yzan, Caldeum
Nobility Sketch + *Diablo III* + Victor Lee

OPPOSITE, BOTTOM RIGHT Barmaid
Sketch + *Diablo III* + Victor Lee

TRAVELING MERCHANT

BODY TATTOO

BRASS ARMBAND
(ONE SIDE)

HAND
SHIELDS.

RIGHT Traveling Merchant Concept +
Diablo III + Victor Lee

OPPOSITE New Tristram Mayor
Concept + *Diablo III* + Victor Lee

FOLLOWING PAGES The Final Stand +
Diablo II + Keith Parkinson

MAYOR FENAN

Diablo

The Lord of Terror awaits you. No matter how confident you are in your past victories, no matter how well you've plundered the depths of countless dungeons for loot, the ultimate test is the confrontation with Diablo himself.

In *Diablo* and *Diablo II*, the Lord of Terror was an intimidating physical presence, a monstrously large creature who radiated raw strength and power and was capable of ripping apart undergeared challengers in a single blow. For *Diablo III*, the artists wanted to dispense with any preconceived notions and push the envelope on what Diablo could look like.

Artists iterated on countless new looks and postures for the Lord of Terror. One early idea from Lead Concept Artist Victor Lee that stuck was a series of mouths on Diablo's shoulders. In the final design, they became the faces of the other Lords of Hell once Diablo has subsumed them as the Prime Evil.

Several other concepts from Lee included imagery that looked like clawed hands grasping Diablo's arms and torso from behind, suggesting that there could be a different, darker power behind the Lord of Terror. Although this detail didn't make it into Diablo's final form, it reemerged as a motif found in later creature designs by Lee, notably for the witch Maghda (see page 159).

The art team generated hundreds of exploratory concepts for Diablo before narrative development decided that Diablo's human host in *Diablo III* would be Leah (see page 70), a young woman. This sparked a new approach to envisioning the Lord of Terror as a more slender creature with feminine features that glowed with the hellfire contained within its body—a defining attribute that would come to influence the designs of the lesser demons found throughout the game.

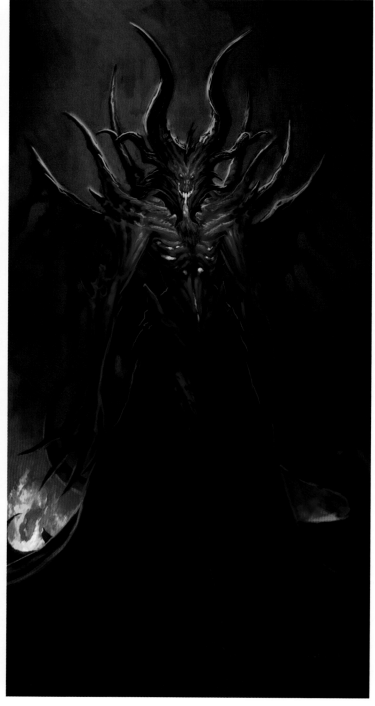

RIGHT Diablo Sketch +
Diablo III + Graven Tung

BELOW Female Diablo Profile Study +
Diablo III + Brian Huang

BELOW RIGHT Diablo Sketch +
Diablo III +Victor Lee

BOTTOM RIGHT Female Diablo Sketch +
Diablo III + Steve Hui

OPPOSITE Female Diablo Concept +
Diablo III Cinematics + Bernie Kang

PHROI

Baal

ABOVE Baal's Insignia + *Diablo Game Manual* + Samwise Didier

BELOW Baal Portrait + *Diablo III* + Sojin Hwang

TOP RIGHT Baal Minion Concept + *Diablo II: Lord of Destruction* + Phil Shenk

BOTTOM RIGHT Baal Concept + *Diablo III* + Victor Lee

Bound beneath the earth for centuries, the Lord of Destruction's escape meant disaster for Sanctuary. In the early *Diablo II* cinematics, Baal inhabited the body of a long-forgotten hero named Tal Rasha, but by the time he was prepared to storm the Ruins of Sescheron, he wore the human's flayed skin as a mask, laying waste to the defenders using his true form—a monstrous, four-legged creature capable of crushing mortal bodies without any effort. Baal is seen again in *Diablo: Immortal*, in an event that shows what he looked like before his capture long ago.

Mephisto

The Lord of Hatred bears one of the most frightening reputations among all the Lords of Hell. As a fearfully effective battle commander, Mephisto was one of the first demons to take interest in Sanctuary, where he found that the minds of mortals were ripe for manipulation. Though he spent centuries sealed beneath the Temple of Light, his mere presence served to corrupt and twist the minds of the Zakarum faithful.

Mephisto's first appearance in *Diablo II* shows only a fraction of his true power, bound as he was to a human host. But what he lacks in size and bulk, he makes up for in power. "He looks like a skeleton torso floating around," Senior Art Director Samwise Didier remembers with a grin. "But then he's got these giant rings of lightning blasting you, and you're like, 'I'm sorry, I didn't mean to make fun of you!'"

ABOVE Sketch of Mephisto Possessing a Follower + *Diablo II* + Uncredited

LEFT Mephisto Concept + *Diablo II* + Anthony Rivero

BELOW LEFT Mephisto Portrait + *Diablo III* + Sojin Hwang

BOTTOM LEFT Mephisto Concept + *Diablo II* + Uncredited

BELOW Mephisto Concept + *Diablo III* + John Polidora

Azmodan

Though all the Lords of Hell fight each other for dominance, the Lord of Sin is one of the most capable strategists in the Eternal Conflict. While his brethren bound themselves to Diablo's plans, Azmodan found power and success scheming against the Lord of Terror. Azmodan was one of the only demons to understand Diablo's plan to ascend as the Prime Evil, and he came closer than anyone to turning that plan in his favor.

Azmodan's design required an incredible amount of iteration before his gargantuan final form was complete. He began as a two-legged melee boss in the mind of Lead Concept Artist Victor Lee, featuring a shark-shaped head that would open up to reveal a grotesque inner face that resembled Azmodan's ultimate visage. This appearance seemed too brutish, though, for one so subtle, and it was later assigned to an appropriately savage demon, Rakanoth, the Lord of Despair.

Meanwhile, the Lord of Sin's form was redesigned to make him a personification of indulgent appetites, with gluttonous folds of flesh and gilded decorations. In this final incarnation, Azmodan's many piercings, scars, and chains also suggest that this Lesser Evil enjoys receiving pain as much as inflicting it.

Belial

Lies have no power unless one wants to believe them. The Lord of Lies found easy prey among the nobility of Kehjistan, promising influence, riches, and countless other fleeting vices, while inhabiting the vessel of the boy emperor Hakan II. But when the heroes of *Diablo III* came to challenge Belial, he discarded the illusion and revealed his true form.

Early concepts show Belial as a powerful battle mage, some of which include unsettling tentacles that look like rabid guard dogs kept on a leash. Later designs focused on expressing his essence as a master of deception. He floats through the air so that he never has to stand on solid ground, and his head has three faces that bear different expressions from different angles.

OPPOSITE Hakan II Concept + *Diablo III* + Victor Lee

ABOVE Belial Sigil + *Diablo III* + Banner Icon

LEFT Belial Sketch + *Diablo III* + Victor Lee

BOTTOM LEFT Belial Sketch + *Diablo III* + Victor Lee

BOTTOM RIGHT Belial Concept + *Diablo III* + Victor Lee

ABOVE Belial Fighting Form Concept +
Diablo III + Sojin Hwang

BELOW & OPPOSITE Belial Concepts +
Diablo III + Victor Lee

Andariel

ABOVE Pentagram Sigil + *Diablo III* + Banner Icon

RIGHT Andariel Concept + *Diablo II* + Phil Shenk

BELOW Andariel Key Art + *Diablo II* + Michael Dashow

The myths of Andariel, the Maiden of Anguish, are frightening and disturbing, telling of a creature able to seduce almost any mortal and inflict unspeakable, lasting horrors upon them when they accept her "gifts." Styled as a temptress, Andariel's feminine in-game design plays with the iconography of succubi, swapping their traditional wings for poison-tipped claws.

When it came to putting together the manual for *Diablo II*, the artists at Blizzard saw an opportunity to develop her demonic character through illustration. "When we did artwork for the manual for Andariel, we pushed her a bit more bestial," recalls Senior Art Director Samwise Didier. "Andariel's a demon, so we wanted to make her a bit more demonic. But that was just in the manual; the game art was already done."

Lilith

Banished for eons yet integral to the history of the Eternal Conflict, the Daughter of Hatred was one of the fabled renegades who created the human world of Sanctuary. And yet, despite her long absence as she languishes in the abyss . . . she shall return. The Mother of Sanctuary will come back to her children, and it shall be a great and terrible day for them all.

Lilith has appeared only briefly in the *Diablo* games, during *Diablo II*'s Pandemonium Event, though her presence has been felt at many points of the story.

Lilith's debut in *Diablo IV* is a reimagining of her form that is far different from her previous appearance (see page 236). Her new design represents "a great example of 'plussing,'" according to Art Director John Mueller, which is a collaborative process during which one artist takes another's concept, affirms what he or she likes about it, and tries to add a cool new idea of his or her own. "Victor Lee did the initial design for Lilith. Then Brom did his own iteration of things and tried different things," says Mueller. "I've always really liked that about any kind of IP: letting really talented artists get ahold of things and then letting them do their version of it. We're doing that with a lot of the characters in the new game."

AB⊕VE Demon Sigil ✦ *Diablo III* ✦ Banner Icon

LEFT Lilith Portrait ✦ *Diablo III* ✦ Sojin Hwang

BEL⊕W Lilith Concept ✦ *Diablo IV* ✦ John Polidora

Tyrael

ABOVE Tyrael Symbol Sketch +
Diablo III + Uncredited

RIGHT & BELOW Fallen Tyrael Armor
Study + *Diablo III* Cinematics +
Joe Peterson

BOTTOM Tyrael Redesign Sketch +
Diablo III Cinematics + Joe Peterson

OPPOSITE Tyrael Redesign Concept +
Diablo III Cinematics + Joe Peterson

The angelic Aspect of Justice and the prime advocate for humanity on the Angiris Council, Tyrael is no stranger to struggle.

Having first appeared in *Diablo II*, Tyrael's primary characteristics—his shining armor, the dark cowl that obscures his face in deep shadow, and his animated wings of wispy light—defined what angels would look like and set a precedent for the other members of the Angiris Council who emerged onscreen in *Diablo III*.

Even though he is humanity's greatest advocate, there is still something unsettling about Tyrael's initial girded form and his lack of a face. "Tyrael's so badass," observes Brom. "Badass and evil sort of overlap. He's not a typical angel; he's not going to sit down with you and hold your hand. Plus, he's just so aesthetically cool. His armor's still got enough of a Gothic flair to it that if you just made his armor black, he could easily be interpreted as on the wicked side of things."

Tyrael, of course, gives up his divinity to become mortal so that he can fulfill his promise to humankind: that they would not face the coming darkness alone. In this incarnation, Tyrael takes on a much more vulnerable, approachable form, although no less noble. An unnamed peasant garbed in rags to start, he grows in stature as heroes emerge who are capable of facing the evil that threatens Sanctuary.

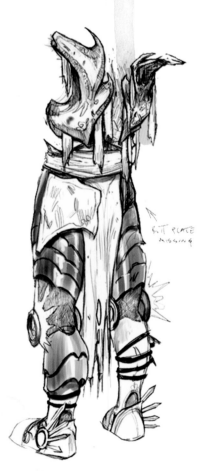

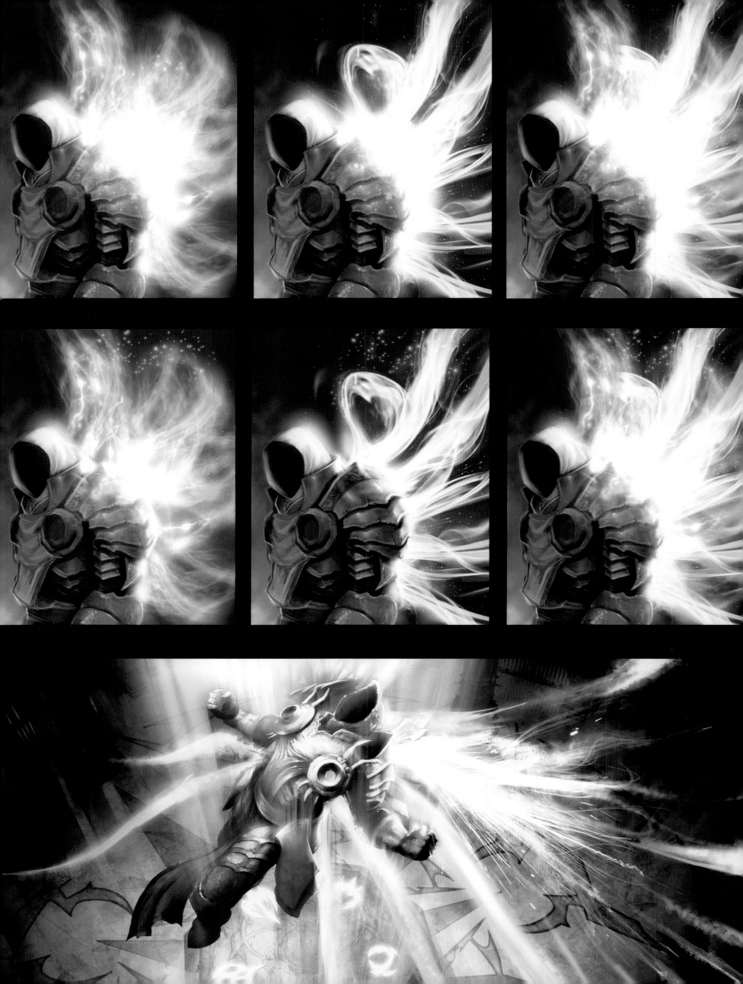

OPPOSITE Tyrael Wing Intensity Studies + *Diablo III* Cinematics + Cinematics Team

ABOVE Tyrael Symbol Sketches + *Diablo III* + Victor Lee

LEFT Fallen Tyrael Sketch + *Diablo III* + Victor Lee

BELOW Fallen Tyrael Concepts + *Diablo III* + Victor Lee

Imperius

ABOVE Sun Sigil + *Diablo III* + Banner Icon

BOTTOM LEFT Imperius's Helm Study + *Diablo III* + Josh Tallman

BOTTOM RIGHT Imperius Concept + *Diablo III* + Josh Tallman

OPPOSITE Imperius Book Cover Art + *Diablo III: Storm of Light* + Laurel Austin

Proud, brave, and stubborn, the Archangel of Valor is a strict martial leader and exemplary warrior. In early versions of the commander of the angels, artists experimented with making his symbol a lion—the fierce king of beasts. As the male lion has a mane around his head that sets him apart from his pride, Imperius wears a helmet and is the only member of the Angiris Council with a traditional angelic halo. However, the animal iconography ultimately did not feel appropriate for the angelic character, so the mane became the corona of a fiery sun with a gleaming circle in the center. This solar crest is repeated in his iconic spear, the head of which looks like the pointed Silver Spire of heaven.

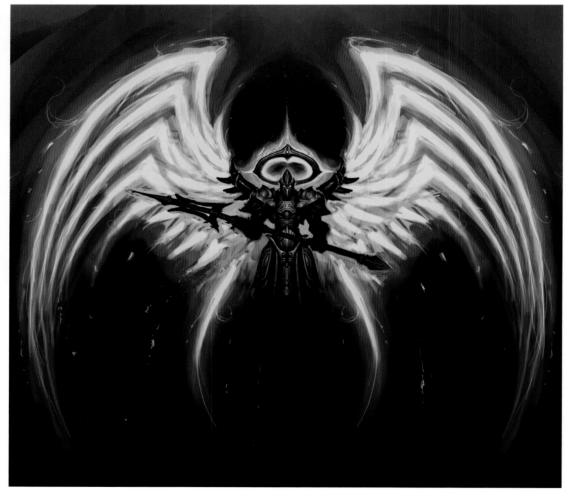

Auriel

Auriel, the Aspect of Hope, leads the chorus of the High Heavens and imbues her fellow angels with a sense of purpose. Without her, the angelic host has little reason to fight when the demon hordes assault heaven in *Diablo III*.

To create a design specific to Auriel that resonated with the precedents set by Tyrael and Imperius, the *Diablo* artists gave her a unique color palette, wing shape, and hood. "From the game cam, an angel's wings are going to be the biggest visual thing you see, so that's one of the best ways to make them separate," explains Senior Concept Artist Josh Tallman.

In the case of Auriel, her wings took on the shape of a heart, conveying the idea that she was vital to the overall spirit of the angels.

OPPOSITE Auriel Concept + *Diablo III* Cinematics + Cinematics Team

ABOVE Auriel's Crest + *Diablo III* + Banner Icon

LEFT Angel of Hope Concept + *Diablo III* + Joe Peterson

BOTTOM LEFT Oracle Angel Concept + *Diablo III* + Victor Lee

BOTTOM RIGHT Auriel Concept + *Diablo III* + Josh Tallman

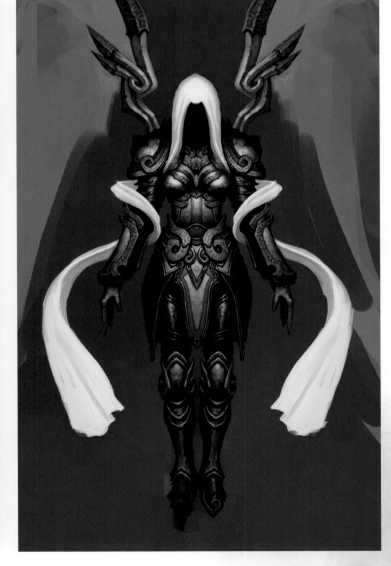

Malthael

ABOVE Malthael Skull Study + *Diablo III: Reaper of Souls* + Banner Icon

BOTTOM LEFT Malthael Sketch + *Diablo III: Reaper of Souls* + Peter Chung

BOTTOM MIDDLE Malthael's Sickles Study + *Diablo III: Reaper of Souls* + Cinematics Team

BOTTOM RIGHT Malthael Concept + *Diablo III: Reaper of Souls* + Josh Tallman

OPPOSITE Malthael Key Art + *Diablo III: Reaper of Souls* + John Polidora

Malthael, the main villain in the *Reaper of Souls* expansion to *Diablo III*, was once the Aspect of Wisdom. Now the Angel of Death, his design is a variation on the iconography of the Grim Reaper. A slim figure draped in black cloth, Malthael wields twin sickles in lieu of the Reaper's traditional scythe. The curves of the blades are repeated in Malthael's armor plating and the patterns on the robes he wears. The lighter-colored ribbons on the end of his cowl contrast markedly against his all-black garb and focus attention on the void where his face should be while giving his fluid movements a haunting, hypnotic quality. These tassels also resemble the stole Christian priests wear when giving Holy Communion, granting his presence a disturbing, spiritual quality.

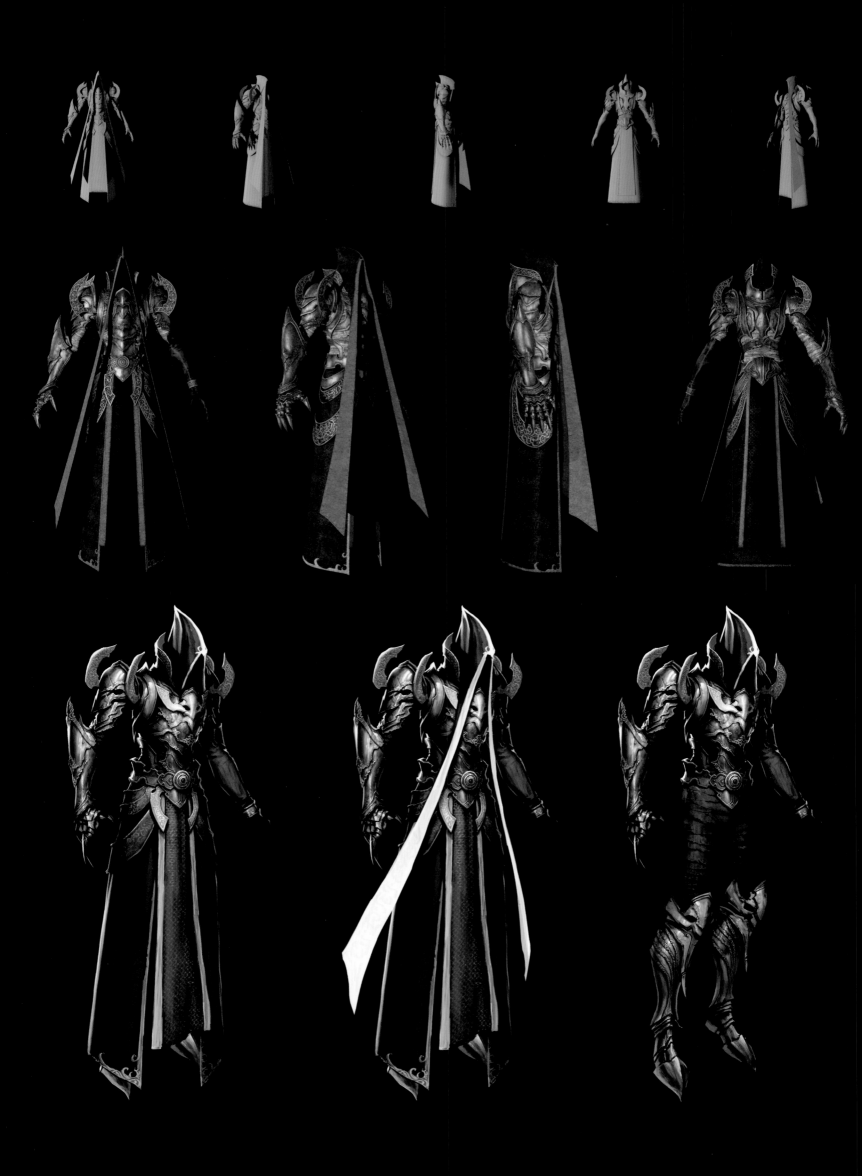

that effect. And if you also look at Catholic priests' robes, it adds a holy-man vibe to it."

—JOSH TALLMAN, Senior Concept Artist

Loot

The core gameplay cycle of Diablo relies heavily on the persistent quest for better and more powerful loot. But the items taken from vanquished foes or harvested from broken barrels aren't just collections of game stats—they also have to look like they belong in the dark, Gothic world of Diablo in order to feel right to an acquiring player.

And there are considerable practical constraints when designing weapons and armor, chiefly because a player typically only sees those key items from the distant isometric perspective of the game camera. Details are often obscured, and strong silhouettes reign supreme. "Whenever we look at anything, it has to be simple, but it also has to feel dark and evil," says Art Director John Mueller.

Finding the right look for a *Diablo* item requires infusing it with some whiff of the demonic or occult. This means lots of jagged edges reminiscent of claws or teeth, evil-looking runes, heavy chains, red glows, black lacquer, bones, and skulls—lots of skulls. Another route to making loot read *Diablo* is to subject it to degradation, using motifs such as tattered cloth and leather, chipped wood, or pitted and rusted metal.

For many, though, the defining loot of the franchise are the red and blue potions from the first two games. "*Diablo* was all about binge-drinking potions," recalls Senior Art Director Samwise Didier. "You're just constantly in the middle of battle drinking these things. I always thought that was funny."

Weapons

ABOVE Weapon Rack Sketch +
Diablo III + Sojin Hwang

RIGHT & BELOW Sword Concepts +
Diablo III + Aaron Gaines

OPPOSITE, TOP, LEFT TO RIGHT
Skycutter Concept + *Diablo III* +
Paul Warzecha | Ghoul King's
Blade Concept, Doombringer
Concept + *Diablo III* + Cory Robinson |
God Butcher Concept + *Diablo III* +
Aaron Gaines

OPPOSITE, BOTTOM, LEFT TO RIGHT
Twisted Blade Concept, Slanderer
Concept + *Diablo III* + Sojin Hwang |
Azurewrath Concept, Devil Wrath
Concept + *Diablo III* + Aaron Gaines

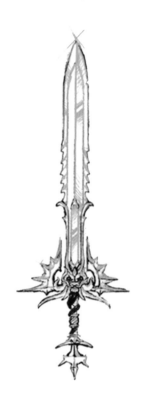

s the tools most classes use to inflict punishment on swarms of enemies in *Diablo*, weapons bear a special significance for players. They are also one of the first things Blizzard artists tackled when developing a signature *Diablo* look.

Senior Art Director Samwise Didier recalls looking at *Diablo* when it was in development and noticing how its in-game weapon sprites were only a few pixels high, barely enough to see more than a weapon's shape and color. As such, the weapons weren't a significant part of the game's visual experience, even though they were huge for gameplay.

But there was a place where the weapons could be made unique and interesting: the user interface. Seizing this opportunity, Blizzard artists made elaborate icons to depict weapons once a player viewed them in their inventory. "They were basically portraits of the weapons," says Didier. "We wanted to impart some flavor. You want people to be excited, not just because of the stats but because of the look of the weapon."

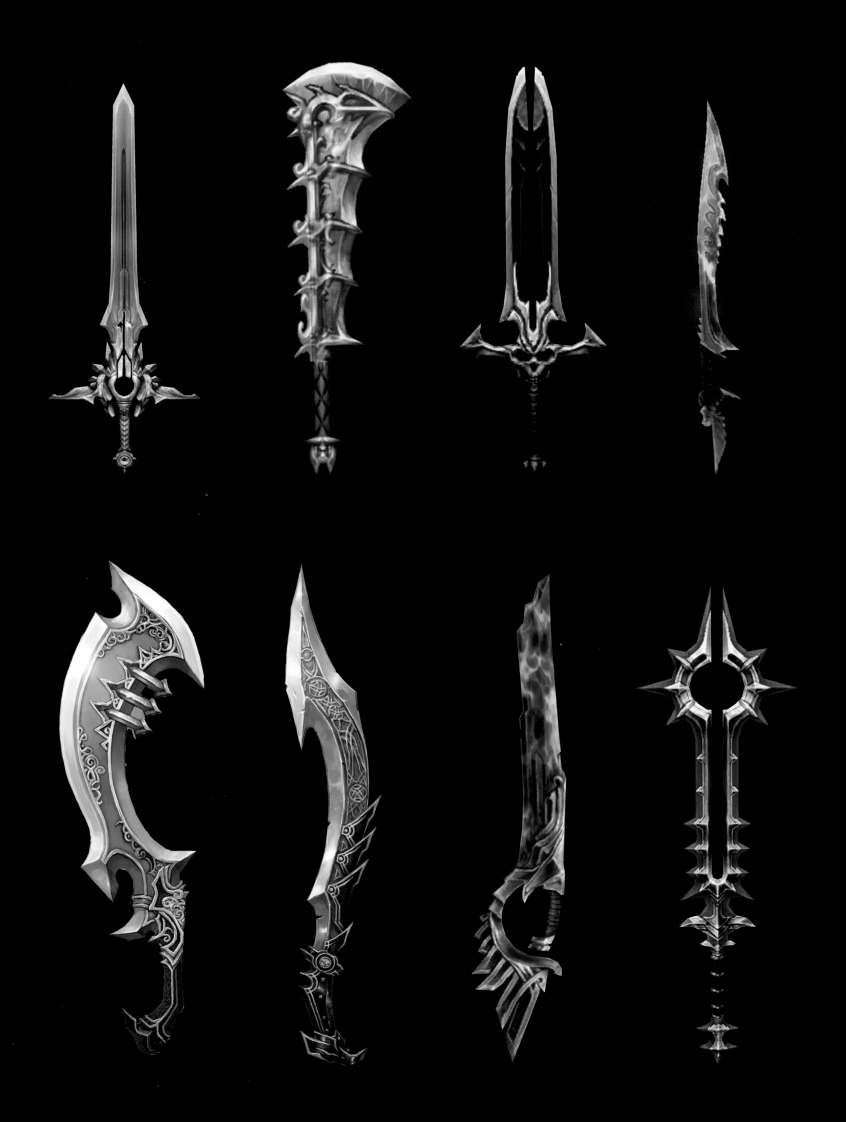

RIGHT Dagger Sketches * Diablo III * Aaron Gaines

BELOW, LEFT TO RIGHT Karleigh's Point Concept, Lord Greenstone's Fan Concept * Diablo III * Sojin Hwang | Veil Piercer Render * Diablo III * Anthony Rivero | Starmetal Kukri Render * Diablo III * Aaron Gaines | Resplendent Scalping Razor Render * Diablo III * Paul Warzecha

ABOVE Fist Weapon Sigil * Diablo III * Banner Icon

RIGHT, CLOCKWISE FROM TOP LEFT Sledge Fist Render * Diablo III * Chris Amaral | Won Khim Lau Render * Diablo III * Paul David | Jawbreaker Concept * Diablo III * Paul David | Demon Claw Render * Diablo III * Sojin Hwang

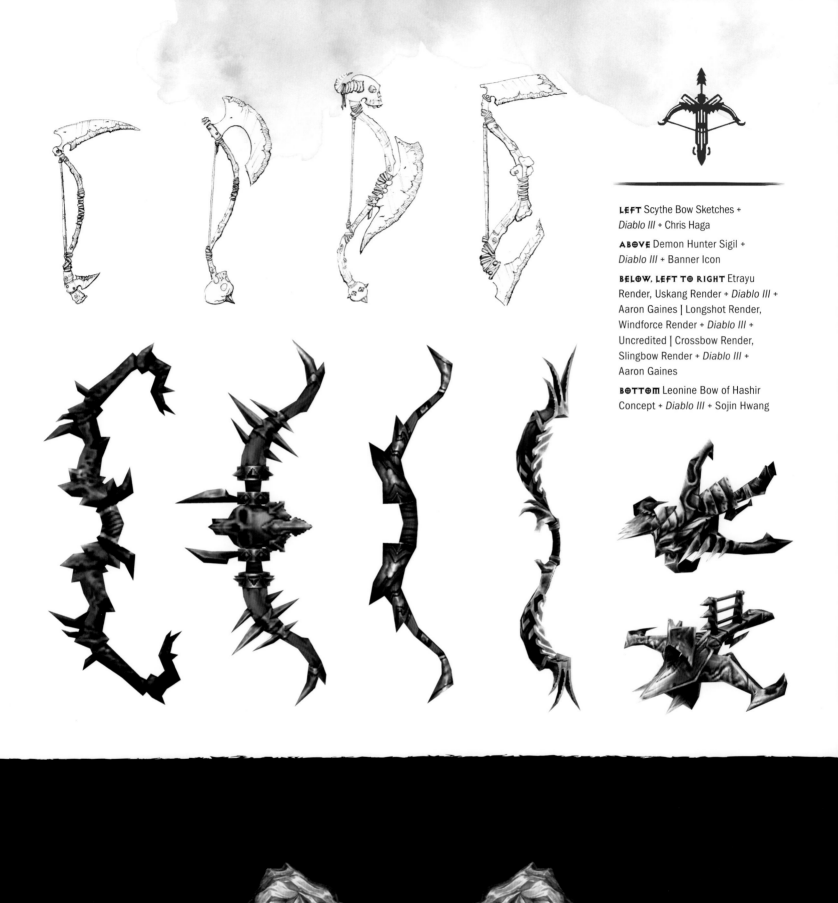

LEFT Scythe Bow Sketches +
Diablo III + Chris Haga

ABOVE Demon Hunter Sigil +
Diablo III + Banner Icon

BELOW, LEFT TO RIGHT Etrayu
Render, Uskang Render + *Diablo III* +
Aaron Gaines | Longshot Render,
Windforce Render + *Diablo III* +
Uncredited | Crossbow Render,
Slingbow Render + *Diablo III* +
Aaron Gaines

BOTTOM Leonine Bow of Hashir
Concept + *Diablo III* + Sojin Hwang

ABOVE Axe Sketch + *Diablo III* + Trent Kaniuga

RIGHT, LEFT TO RIGHT Aidan's Revenge Concept + *Diablo III* + Aaron Gaines | Flesh Tearer Concept, Sky Splitter Concept + *Diablo III* + Tyson Murphy

BELOW, LEFT TO RIGHT Cinder Switch Concept + *Diablo III* + Chris Haga | Heavy Axe Concept, Skartaran Axe Concept + *Diablo III* + Tyson Murphy | Butcher's Cleaver Concept + *Diablo III* + Paul David

BOTTOM, LEFT TO RIGHT Skorn Concept, King Maker Concept + *Diablo III* + Aaron Gaines | Blade of the Tribes Concept + *Diablo III* + Paul David | Hack Concept + *Diablo III* + Uncredited

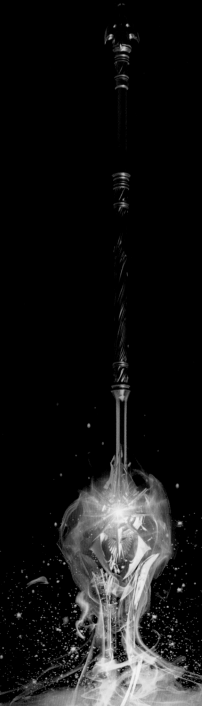

LEFT Spear and Polearm Sketches + *Diablo III* + Victor Lee

BELOW LEFT, LEFT TO RIGHT Bovine Bardiche Concept + *Diablo III* + Anthony Rivero | Akanesh Concept + *Diablo III* + Aaron Gaines | The Herald of Righteousness Concept + *Diablo III* + Cory Robinson | Man Prodder Concept + *Diablo III* + Josh Tallman

BELOW Solarion, Imperius's Spear FX Study + *Diablo III* Cinematics + Cinematics Team

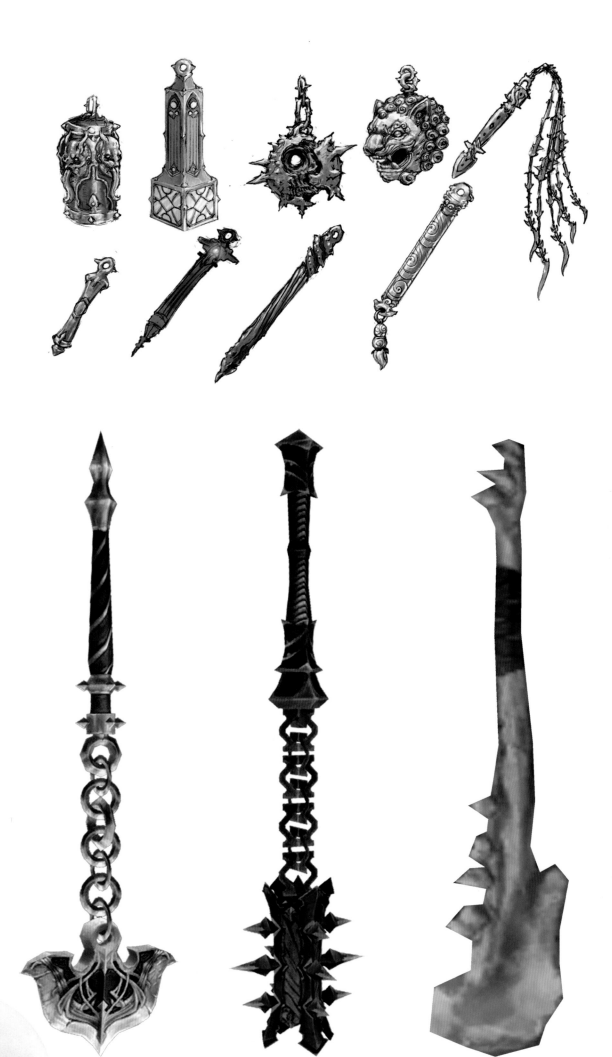

LEFT Suwong Diviner Staff Sketches + *Diablo III* + Victor Lee

ABOVE Witch Doctor Sigil + *Diablo III* + Banner Icon

BELOW, LEFT TO RIGHT Staff Concepts + *Diablo III* + Josh Tallman | Valthek's Rebuke Concept, Spear of Lycander Concept, Smoldering Core Concept + *Diablo III* + Sojin Hwang

Armor

rmor becomes especially important—both for players and for the *Diablo* artists—when you get to the class sets. "That's where we tend to have the most fun," says Art Director John Mueller. "That's when it really gets into the class fantasy of it."

Conceptualizing class-specific armor sets usually begins with materials. The Monk, for example, has armor sets created mainly from cloth and leather. Additionally, class-specific armor has to play within the boundaries established by a distinctive class silhouette. So Demon Hunter sets tend to read slim and formfitting, while Barbarian sets have prominent shoulder pads. Finally, there has to be a thematic hook to the class, such as the Necromancer's sets featuring blood, bone, and organs or the Witch Doctor's sets including feathers, skulls, wood, or other materials that the hero might use when casting his or her distinctive spells.

"There's a logic behind it. You have to have that, even if it is magical," says Concept Artist Trent Kaniuga. "In *Diablo*, armor has to look like it's crafted by a blacksmith or by a wizard from the existing world."

OPPOSITE, CLOCKWISE FROM TOP
LEFT Lidless Wall Concept + *Diablo III* + Aaron Gaines | Sacred Shield Concept + *Diablo III* + Anthony Rivero | Jekangbord Concept, Eberli Charo Concept, Vo'Toyias Spiker Concept + *Diablo III: Reaper of Souls* + Victor Lee
ABOVE Shield Sigil + *Diablo III* + Banner Icon
LEFT Jekangbord Sketch + *Diablo III: Reaper of Souls* + Victor Lee
BELOW Stormshield Concept + *Diablo III* + Paul David
BOTTOM Eberli Charo Sketches + *Diablo III: Reaper of Souls* + Victor Lee

OPPOSITE Carnevil Concept + *Diablo III* + Sojin Hwang

LEFT The Magistrate Concepts + *Diablo III* + Sojin Hwang

ABOVE Khassetti Death Mask Concept + *Diablo III* + Sojin Hwang

BELOW LEFT Wizard Stechhelm Study + *Diablo III* + Sojin Hwang

BELOW Wizard Light Helm Study + *Diablo III* + Victor Lee

"It's very important, when you're doing an armor set, to have an iconic, one-sentence description like, 'That's the one with the raven theme.' Or 'That's the one that's like Anubis.' Otherwise, it doesn't have a cohesive identity."

—TRENT KANIUGA, Concept Artist

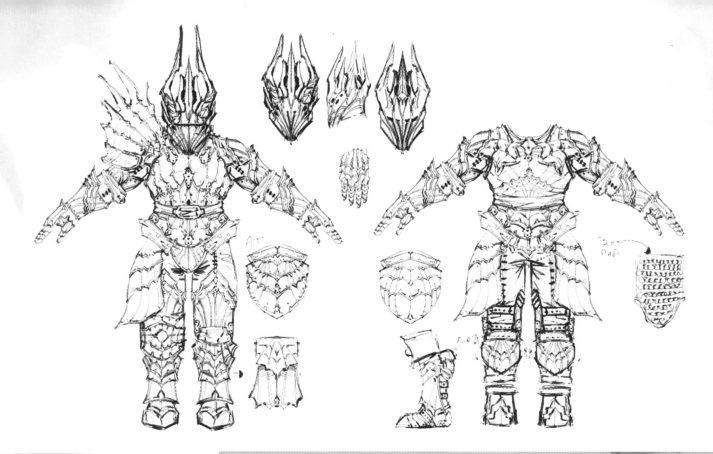

ABOVE Human Armor Sketches +
Diablo III + Aaron Gaines

RIGHT Female Wizard Stone Armor
Sketch + *Diablo III* + Josh Tallman

BELOW Stone Armor Sketch +
Diablo III + Josh Tallman

OPPOSITE Mage Concepts +
Diablo III + Victor Lee

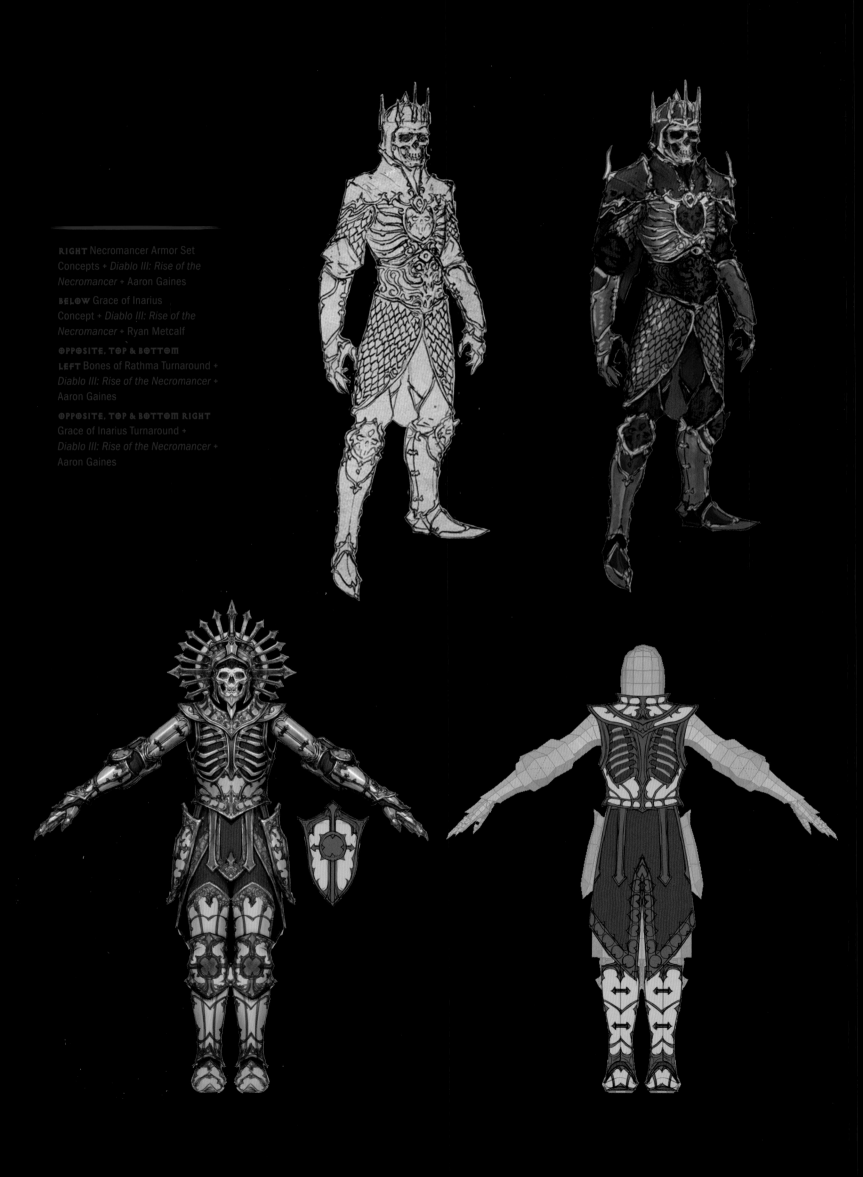

RIGHT Necromancer Armor Set Concepts + *Diablo III: Rise of the Necromancer* + Aaron Gaines

BELOW Grace of Inarius Concept + *Diablo III: Rise of the Necromancer* + Ryan Metcalf

OPPOSITE, TOP & BOTTOM LEFT Bones of Rathma Turnaround + *Diablo III: Rise of the Necromancer* + Aaron Gaines

OPPOSITE, TOP & BOTTOM RIGHT Grace of Inarius Turnaround + *Diablo III: Rise of the Necromancer* + Aaron Gaines

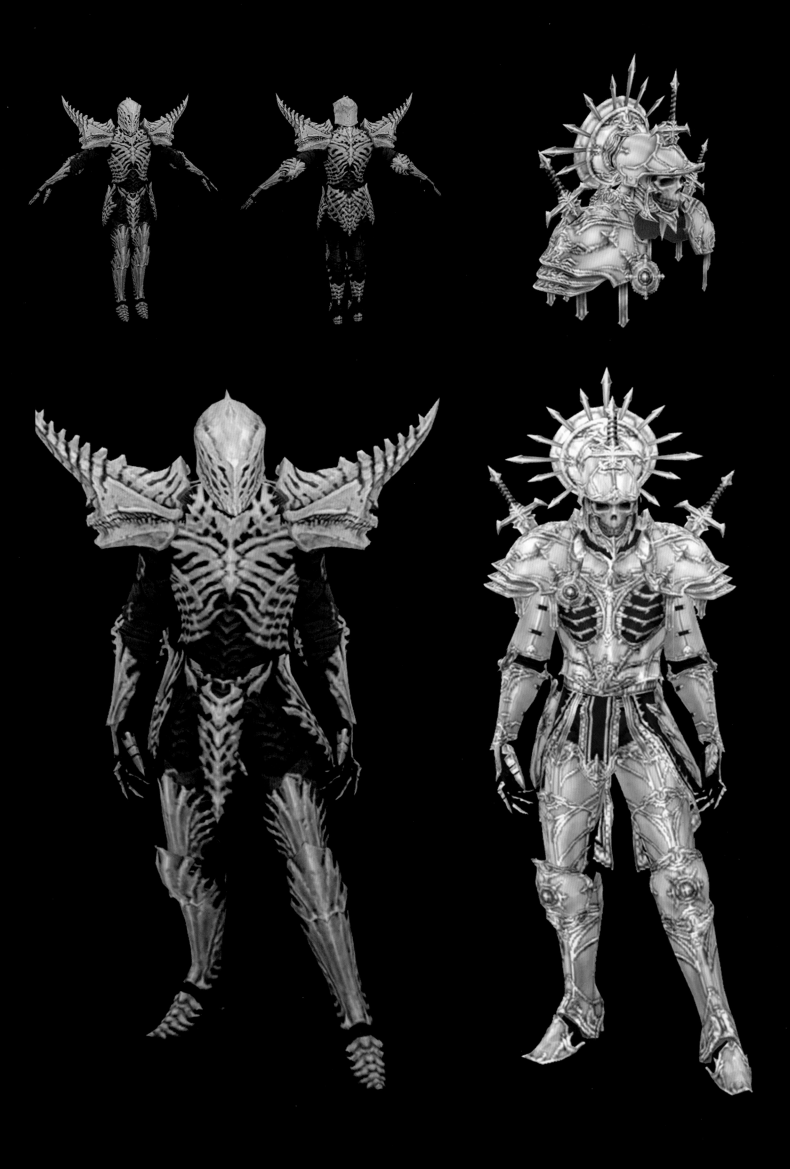

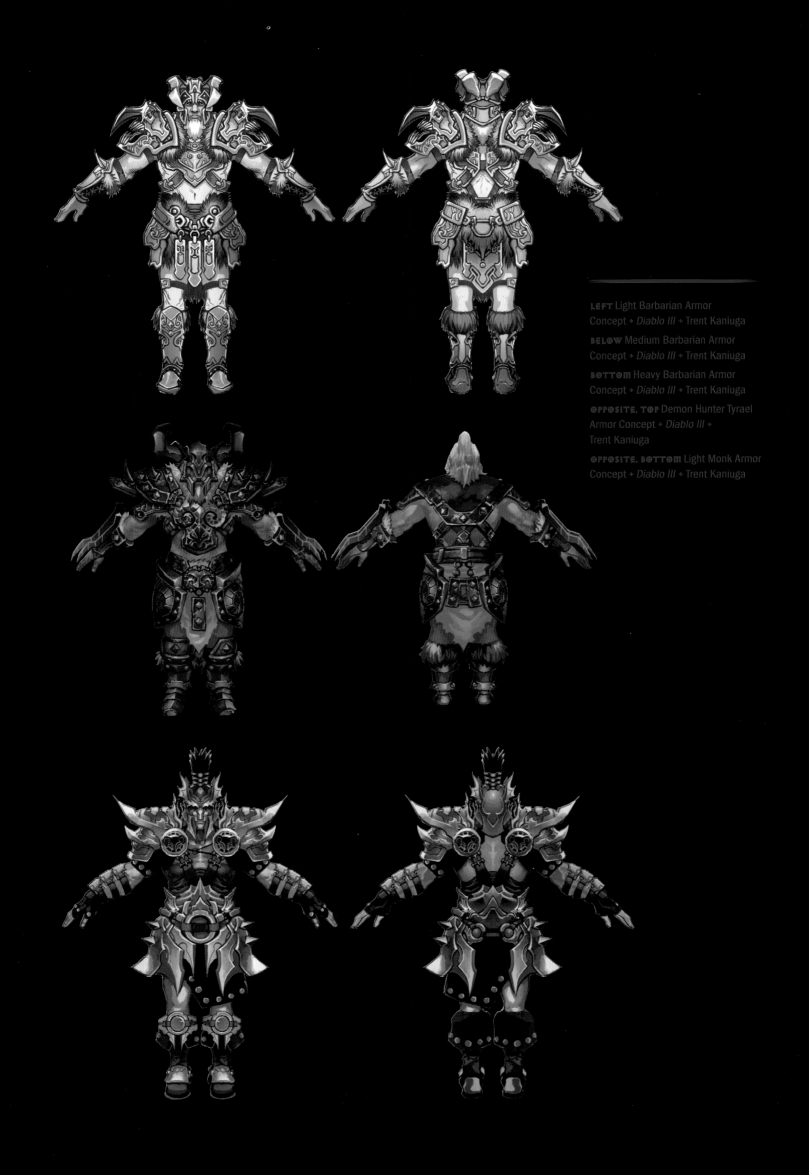

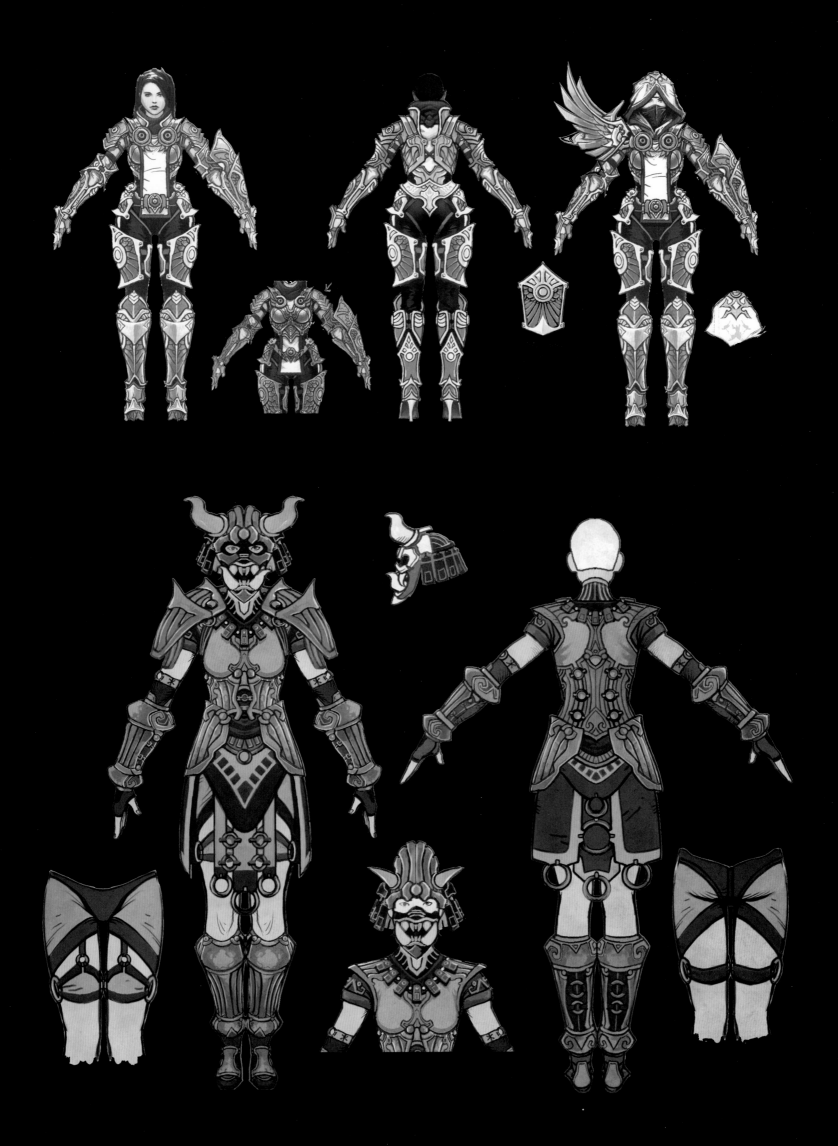

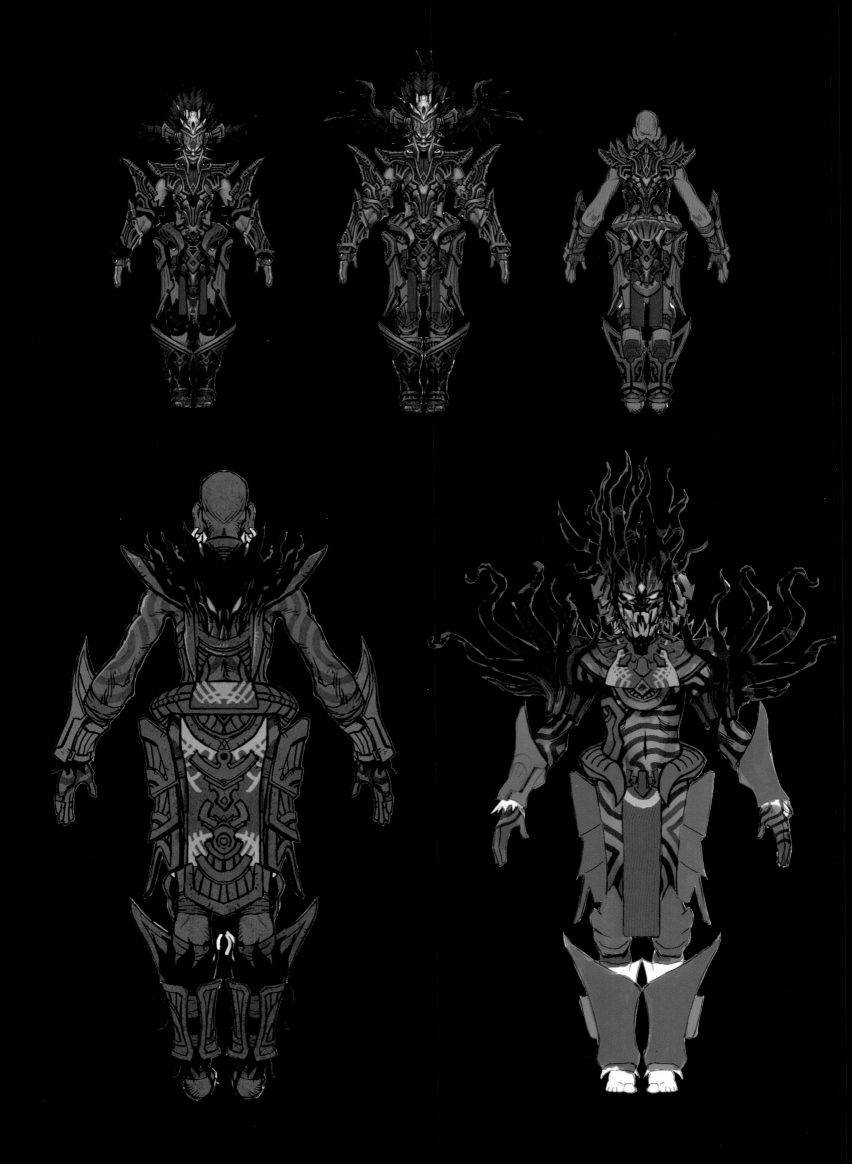

THESE PAGES Heavy Witch Doctor Armor
Concepts + *Diablo III* + Trent Kaniuga

Other Items

ABOVE Inkwell Sketch +
Diablo III + Uncredited

BELOW Flag Sketches +
Diablo III + Victor Lee

OPPOSITE, TOP Totem Sketches +
Diablo III + Trent Kaniuga

OPPOSITE, BOTTOM LEFT Banner
Sketches + *Diablo III* + Trent Kaniuga

OPPOSITE, BOTTOM RIGHT Pole
Sketches + *Diablo III* + Uncredited

esides armor and weapons, the world of *Diablo* is full of other objects that players can interact with. Most are part of the environments where they appear, but some can be acquired by heroes or are strongly associated with them. One special type of item is the banner the artists designed for each class. "We did it in every single game we've done," observes Senior Art Director Samwise Didier. "It's basically just one more thing that we could do to link people to something, without having to have them read this gigantic whole story. It goes back to every country has a flag, every sort of military group has its thing, every soccer team or football team has their logo."

DARK OLD METAL

GOLD COLOR

IKON

FABR

ATTACHED TO
BACK OF TROOPS
OR CREATURE
TROOPS ARE RIDIN

fabric
WRAPPING

WOOD.

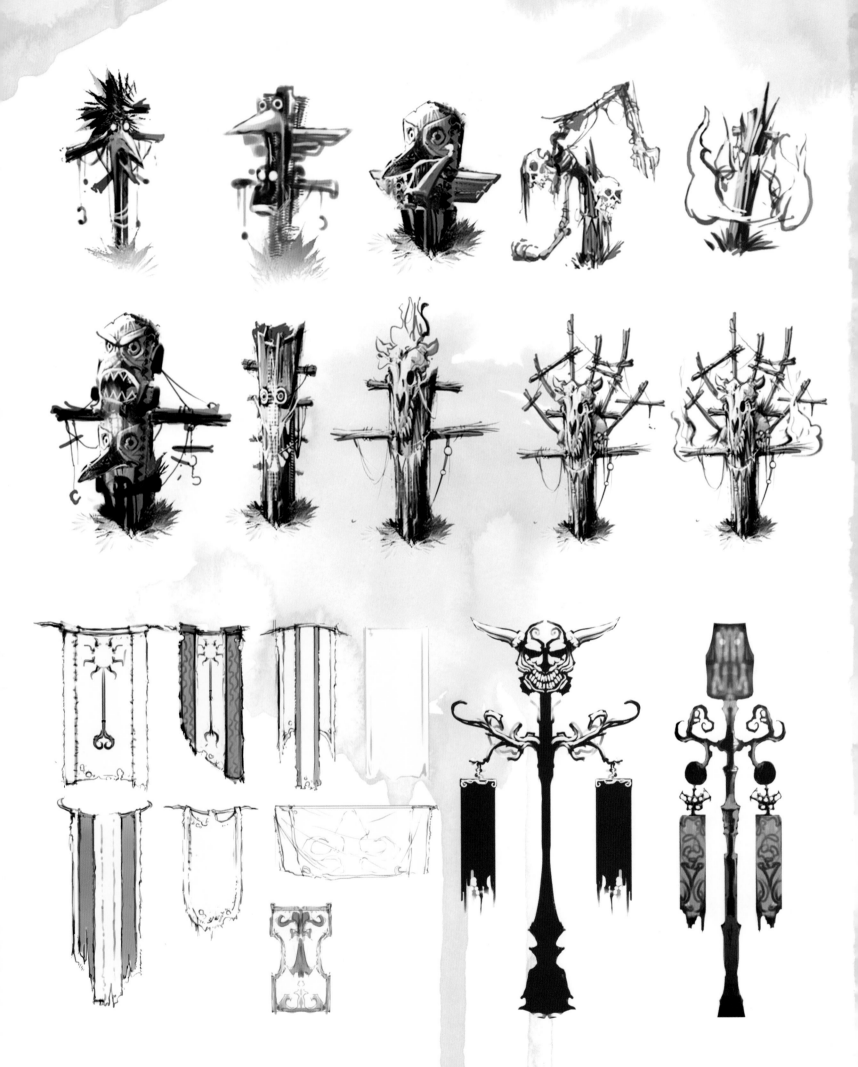

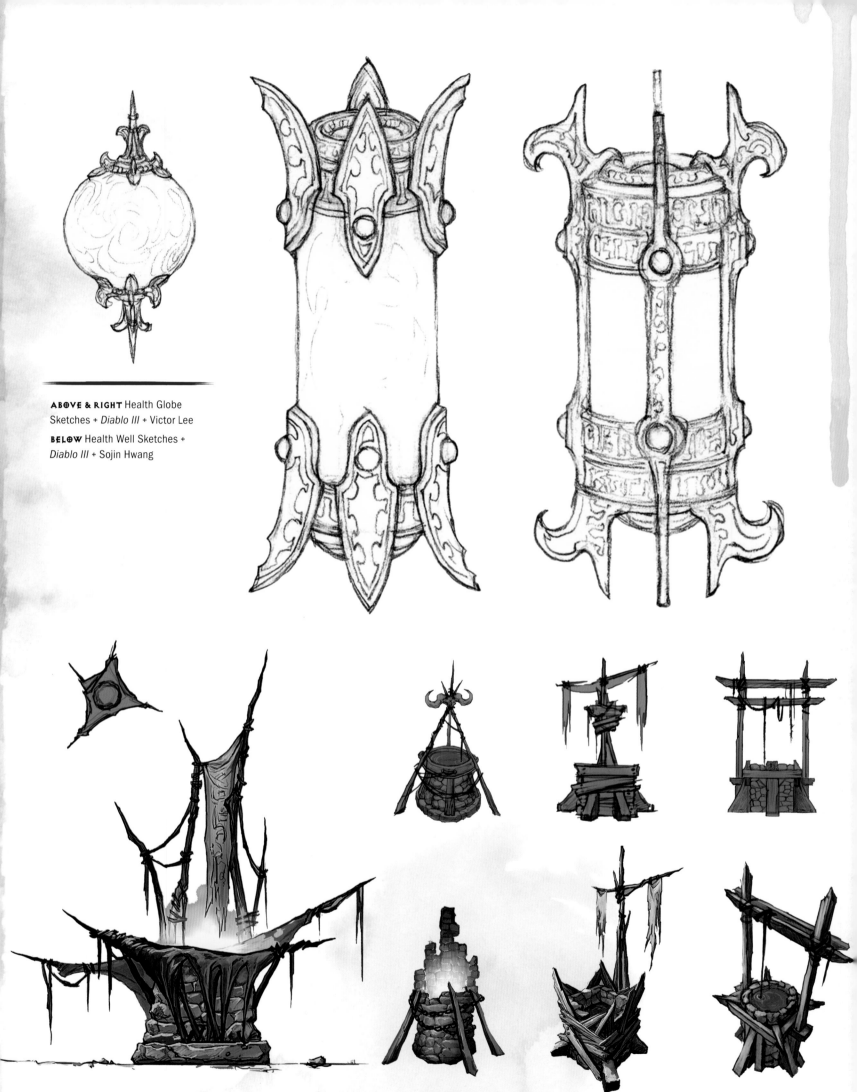

ABOVE & RIGHT Health Globe Sketches + *Diablo III* + Victor Lee

BELOW Health Well Sketches + *Diablo III* + Sojin Hwang

LEFT Throne Lighting Study + *Diablo III* Cinematics + Chris Thunig

BELOW Black Soulstone Lighting Displacement Study + *Diablo III* Cinematics + Bernie Kang

Creatures

While the heroes get a lot of attention from players, the monsters of Diablo are often the favorites among the artists because they present more possibilities for creativity. The move from the deep dungeon beneath Tristram to the larger world of Sanctuary in Diablo II was especially exciting, as it offered many more opportunities to explore a wide range of natural and unnatural creatures. "When you're just in a dungeon, you're kind of stuck with a lot of the standard dungeon things—skeletons and zombies, and all that. But when you're able to go to a whole other tile set, you can branch out and create new things," comments Senior Art Director Samwise Didier.

Lead Concept Artist Victor Lee, who has designed more *Diablo* monsters than anyone else, says he tries to create real empathy and interesting traits for the creatures he envisions. Lee builds up a monster using four guideposts: 1) silhouette, 2) volume, 3) palette, and 4) grouping. The *silhouette* is the outline of the creature, which makes it instantly recognizable in the fast-paced gameplay of *Diablo*. *Volume* is how much space a monster takes up and how heavy it is. *Palette* is the set of colors that will give a monster an appropriate level of contrast with the environment where it will appear. Lastly, *grouping* means creating distinction between key parts of a creature, such as its arms and torso, so that they can be clearly perceived during the game.

But creating a strong creature design isn't just a matter of following these guideposts. "A lot of times when I do a design, I know what the 'normal' thing to do is and I try to flip it," says Lee. "'Is there a way to do it that's not normal; is there a different way to do it; is there a counterintuitive way to do this?' All to get something fresh—something we might not have seen before."

The Skeleton King

ABOVE Skeleton King Sigil ∗ *Diablo III* ∗ Banner Icon **RIGHT** Skeleton King Model ∗ *Diablo III* ∗ Paul David

BELOW Skeleton King Head Study ∗ *Diablo III* ∗ Josh Tallman

BOTTOM LEFT Skeleton King Sketch ∗ *Diablo III* ∗ Josh Tallman

BOTTOM RIGHT Skeleton King Concept ∗ *Diablo III* ∗ Josh Tallman

OPPOSITE Skeleton King ∗ *Diablo III* ∗ Brom

King Leoric chose the small town of Tristram to be the seat of his rule, and in so doing, he sealed his own fate. The Lord of Terror was imprisoned beneath that land, and Leoric soon succumbed to madness. After being executed by his knights, Leoric rises as the Skeleton King in *Diablo*, is defeated by the heroes in that story, and then is reawakened by the falling star in *Diablo III*.

An iconic *Diablo* character, the Skeleton King was painted by Brom using a muted, sophisticated color palette appropriate to an undead warrior who dwells deep below the earth in a dark crypt. "I was given ten or twenty wonderful, different versions of it, and I cobbled together the elements that I liked best," recalls Brom. "Those colors, getting those painterly colors into the game is a great goal. Muted doesn't mean that it's less brilliant. In some ways, it makes it more brilliant, the more sophisticated colors playing off each other."

The Butcher

The Butcher made his first unforgettable appearance in *Diablo* with the dreaded phrase "Fresh meat." Revisiting the iconic demon's design for *Diablo III*, the artists realized their memories of the larger-than-life demon were vastly disproportionate to the actual sprite in the first game.

"The character was small on the screen," recalls Art Director John Mueller. "If you think about *Diablo* and the graphics at the time, my imagination filled in so much of it. It definitely left an imprint. I feel like I should probably try to draw that at some point. Like what was I actually thinking about when I first experienced that?"

Lead Concept Artist Victor Lee tried to give the revived Butcher added gravitas by designing a den that features a throne made out of a flayed demon carcass, suggesting that the Butcher likes to kill bigger fiends to furnish his lair with unique décor made of bone, flesh, and skin.

Maghda

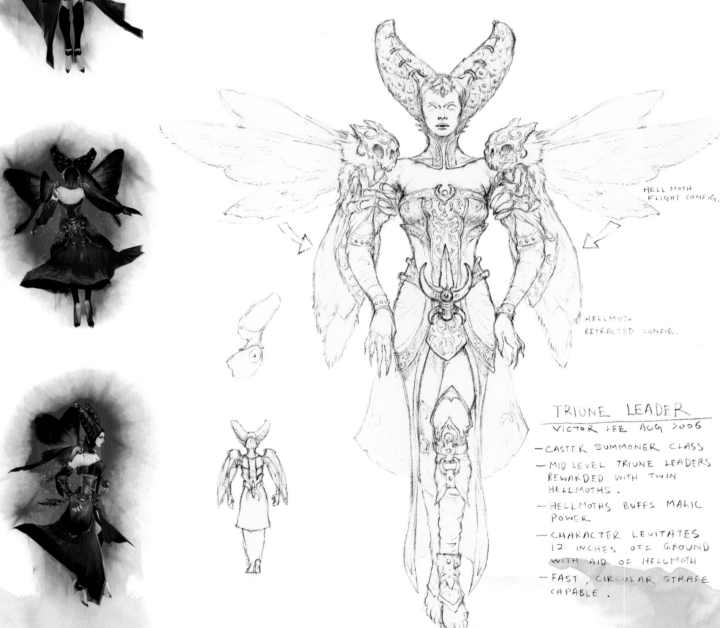

Maghda, leader of the Coven, needed to be extra colorful to separate her from the orange-hued desert arena where players confront her in Act II of *Diablo III*, according to Lead Concept Artist Victor Lee. An airborne caster, Maghda can't fly on her own—she relies on a pair of moths to keep her afloat. Equipped with real skulls (versus mere death's-head patterns) in early ideations by Lee, the moths have eyes on their wings that are reminiscent of the ones he experimented with for Diablo's design (see page 90). And the claws the moths use to hold Maghda's arms recall the "grasping hands" motif the artist also explored during early iterations of Diablo, suggesting that some greater power may have a hold over the witch and the Coven.

OPPOSITE Triune Cultist Leader Concept + *Diablo III* + Victor Lee

ABOVE Maghda Sigil + *Diablo III* + Banner Icon

LEFT Maghda Turnaround + *Diablo III* + Paul David

BELOW Triune Cultist Leader Sketch + *Diablo III* + Victor Lee

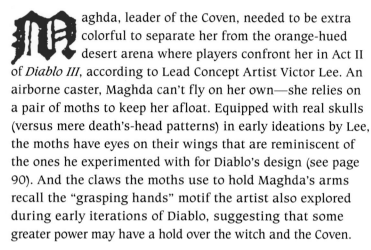

HELL MOTH FLIGHT CONFIG.

HELLMOTH RETRACTED CONFIG.

TRIUNE LEADER
VICTOR LEE AUG 2006

- CASTER SUMMONER CLASS
- MID LEVEL TRIUNE LEADERS REWARDED WITH TWIN HELLMOTHS.
- HELLMOTHS BUFFS MAGIC POWER
- CHARACTER LEVITATES 12 INCHES OFF GROUND WITH AID OF HELLMOTH
- FAST, CIRCULAR STRAFE CAPABLE.

Zoltun Kulle

Once one of the most powerful mages in Sanctuary and a founding member of the Horadrim, Zoltun Kulle gave in to the temptations of dark magic and was executed by his brethren. Kulle's most powerful transgression was creating the Black Soulstone, which could hold the souls of many beings at once, including demons, angels, and even the seven Great Evils.

Kulle's archive, where he conducted his forbidden research, lies buried to the east of Caldeum. There, his earthbound head reanimated and created a new body held together by sand. "All of his spells needed to be wrapped up in this sand element," recalls Concept Artist Trent Kaniuga. "The sand holds his body together, and you can see some of that in those concepts, where it's swooshing and swirling around him."

Despite multiple concepts depicting Kulle as a venerable old wizard who was almost priestlike, the final concept selected was a quick doodle sketched by Kaniuga. "It's the silhouette," he remarks. "The doodles are where the ideas come across in a way that works well with the game design, the gameplay, and the player's experience. That's often where the real gem is."

OPPOSITE Zoltun Kulle Concept • *Diablo III* • Trent Kaniuga

ABOVE Zoltun Kulle Sigil • *Diablo III* • Banner Icon

LEFT Zoltun Skeleton Mage Sketch • *Diablo III* • Victor Lee

BOTTOM LEFT Zoltun Kulle Concept • *Diablo III* • Trent Kaniuga

BOTTOM RIGHT Zoltun Kulle Sketch • *Diablo III* • Trent Kaniuga

Siegebreaker Assault Beast

The Siegebreaker Assault Beast is a pure expression of brutality with its formidable size, heavy iron plates, and intimidating spikes. But the blinded beast is also one of the deepest studies of the pain demons have to endure as part of their existence in the world of *Diablo*, per Lead Concept Artist Victor Lee. Held at bay by chains attached to spikes driven into its body, the Siegebreaker must tear itself free, rending its flesh, in order to attack. Lee's defining concept includes a lower body like a bulldog's, emphasizing the Siegebreaker's tenacity, and a master that rides on the beast's head, suggesting that it's been trained to be vicious rather than being utterly savage by nature.

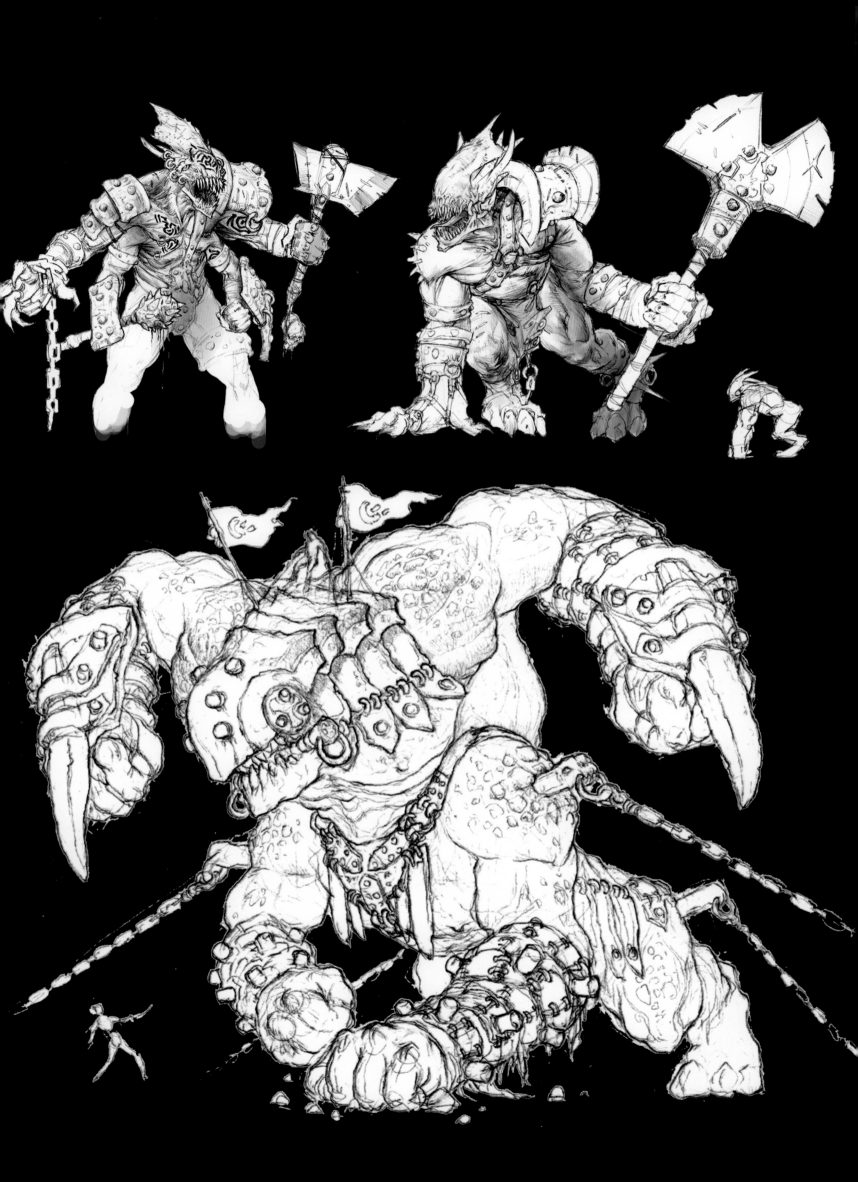

Cydaea

The disturbing yet alluring consort to the Lord of Sin, Cydaea almost didn't make it into *Diablo III*. Early concepts sparked concerns that the Maiden of Lust would be too complex to model in time for the game's release, but the fan response to her reveal at BlizzCon 2009 pushed the team to make sure she made an appearance. Cydaea shares grotesque traits with Azmodan, juxtaposing spider legs with a beautiful woman's torso in an unsettling arrangement. Her corset, veil, and gloves speak to pretensions of a certain courtly refinement—as well as a willingness to experiment with pleasure and pain.

OPPOSITE Mistress of Pain Concept + *Diablo III* + Victor Lee

ABOVE Mistress of Pain Sigil + *Diablo III* + Banner Icon

LEFT Lust Sketch + *Diablo III* + Nathan Bowden

BELOW Mistress of Pain Concept + *Diablo III* + Victor Lee

Angels

Contrary to most depictions of angelic beings in our world, the angels of the High Heavens feel little affinity for humans. More often than not, angels are indifferent to humanity and the role it may play in the Eternal Conflict. "To me, an angel is just another kind of monster," says Lead Concept Artist Victor Lee. "They should be aloof. In my mind, they are at another level of existence. I really don't see angels chatting with humans; they are a different species."

Lee's early angel designs for *Diablo III* featured impassive faces before cowls and impenetrable shadows became hard guidelines, making facelessness a defining feature of angelhood. "It is actually pretty challenging to design a character without a face, because humans relate to faces very easily," says Lee. "Without a face to work with, you have to rely on other things."

Following the lead of Tyrael, who first appeared in *Diablo II* and provided the model for future angel designs, wings made of wisps of light became the most important mechanisms of expression for the angelic hosts' faceless, heavily armored forms.

GAUNLET OPENS
FOR SLIT-SECOND
BEFORE SNAPPING
SHUT TO FIRE
OFF SPELLS.

Reapers

Until *Reaper of Souls*, angels had never been enemies to the Heroes of Sanctuary. But for Malthael's assault on all of humanity, the artists of the *Diablo* team were given a chance to explore how the forces of the High Heavens could become adversaries. The final designs for the fallen-angel Reapers take cues from Malthael's design, with lithe forms, pointed headgear, and curved armor plates and blades. Meanwhile, undead Reapers animated from the dead of Westmarch by Malthael and his minions resemble armored banshees and ghosts.

A previous Reaper concept by Lead Concept Artist Victor Lee depicted a much more gruesome, savage type of creature with a different purpose. "His job is basically to assassinate angels, and he does that with that tusk hammer of his. And he wears angel corpses on his wings, which, after you beat on him enough, he will rip off and use as dual katanas." In the final release of *Diablo III*, this early Reaper design became the basis for the Corrupted Angels encountered in Act IV.

Beasts

onsters classified as beasts really came into their own in *Diablo II*, where players began to explore the world of Sanctuary beyond Tristram. The category includes everything from oversized vermin such as spiders, wasps, and worms to pure inventions such as Quill Fiends, Khazra, and Lacuni.

When designing beasts, *Diablo* artists are careful not to make them seem too mindless so that a player can potentially experience a certain degree of disturbing identification with their foes. "My thinking is if I design a monster that's just purely like a beast, then it's kind of hard for people to relate to it," says Lead Concept Artist Victor Lee. "If I incorporate some human elements and human forms into the design, I feel like it connects better with people. People find it a little bit easier to relate to designs that they're familiar with. And it's easier to creep them out that way."

OPPOSITE Mutated Goatman Concept + *Diablo III* + Josh Tallman

ABOVE Beast Monster Sigil + *Diablo III* + Banner Icon

BELOW Blood Hawk Nest Sketch + *Diablo III* + Mark Gibbons

SENTRY RAISES THE ALARM.

HAWKS HAVE 'HIJACKED' A WOOD WRAITH + BUILT THEIR NEST OVER ITS TRUNK — COULD BE STATIONARY OR LUMBER AROUND BLINDLY.

NORDIC GOAT

NORDIC BOAR

NORDIC MELEE BEAST

BLOWHOLE

ABOVE Nordic Goat Sketch +
Diablo III + Victor Lee

ABOVE RIGHT Nordic Boar Sketch +
Diablo III + Victor Lee

RIGHT Nordic Melee Beast Sketch +
Diablo III + Victor Lee

LEFT Gnarled Walker Concept +
Diablo III + Mark Gibbons

BELOW Mutated Goatmen Sketch +
Diablo III + Josh Tallman

RIGHT Sand Golem Concept + *Diablo III* + Trent Kaniuga

BELOW Dune Thresher Concept + *Diablo III* + Mark Gibbons

OPPOSITE, TOP Shadow Vermin Sketch + *Diablo III* + Josh Tallman

OPPOSITE, BOTTOM Serpentis Concept + *Diablo III* + Mark Gibbons

Demons

The classic image of a demon is a red or black smooth-skinned humanoid with wings, claws, and sharp teeth, surrounded by fire when in their native hell. While many of the early iterations of demons in *Diablo* and *Diablo II*—such as Balrogs, Succubi, and the Fallen—cleaved to these conventions, concept artists working on *Diablo III* set out to upend them. One key idea was to take the fire of hell and put it inside new demons, such as Flay Demons and Mallet Lords, giving them an unnerving, perpetual glow from within that speaks to their hellish origins and power. "The thinking is that instead of them being on fire, what if demons are basically mobile containers of hellfire that they bring into battle when they cross the realms?" comments Lead Concept Artist Victor Lee. "They contain a little bit of hell in each of them."

"You can only have so many brutes who bludgeon you. Anything that can add a new wrinkle to combat—a bizarre silhouette or an imaginative special effect—is welcome in a game where you literally kill untold numbers of hell spawn."

—PHROILAN GARDNER, Senior Artist

OPPOSITE Serpent Magus + *Diablo III* + Brom

BELOW LEFT Rattler Mage Sketch + *Diablo III* + Victor Lee

BELOW MIDDLE Dominatrix Sketch + *Diablo III* + Mark Gibbons

BELOW RIGHT Subjugator Sketch + *Diablo III* + Victor Lee

BOTTOM Enslaved Nightmare Concept + *Diablo III* + Victor Lee

FOLLOWING PAGES Fallen Army Key Art + *Diablo III* + Phroilan Gardner

"There are two kinds of thinking. I don't think it's a negative thing. We keep each other in check. Like, 'Are we going too dark? Are we going too colorful? Are we going too stylized?' We're constantly having these push-and-pull discussions that sometimes slow things down, but I think it's a pretty healthy thing to have."

—VICTOR LEE, Lead Concept Artist

ABOVE Lanzuul's Minion Concept + *Diablo III* + Victor Lee

BELOW Demon Sketch + *Diablo III* + Josh Tallman

BELOW RIGHT Demon Sketch + *Diablo III* + Steve Hui

OPPOSITE Balrog Concept + *Diablo III* + Victor Lee

OPPOSITE, TOP Mallet Lord Concept + *Diablo III* + Victor Lee

OPPOSITE, BOTTOM Winged Demon Concept + *Diablo III* + Steve Hui

LEFT Simian Demon Warrior Concept + *Diablo III* + Joe Peterson

ABOVE Trench Demon Concept + *Diablo III* + Bernie Kang

BELOW Demon Sketch + *Diablo III* + Bernie Kang

FOLLOWING PAGES Demon Pit Concept + *Diablo III* + Victor Lee

Undead

ABOVE Zombie Sketch +
Diablo III + Uncredited

RIGHT Zombie Concept +
Diablo II + Uncredited

BELOW Zombie Spider Sketches +
Diablo III + Trent Kaniuga

BOTTOM Zombie Studies +
Diablo III + Trent Kaniuga

OPPOSITE Undead Warrior Concept +
Diablo III + Cole Eastburn

The undead are some of the most enduring adversaries in *Diablo*, having been front and center since the first level of *Diablo*'s cathedral dungeon. A byproduct of the Burning Hell's growing influence in Sanctuary, undead can be drafted as monsters in any zone where there might be buried bodies. Because of this, *Diablo* artists try to give each undead creature a strong location-specific design, which also helps them avoid the generic skeleton and zombie clichés of popular culture. "If everything is just this brownish, bleak skeleton monster that has all these oozing sores all over, that gets boring after the fifth one," observes Senior Art Director Samwise Didier.

"We get to try a lot of different things, and we get to experiment, and we get to do visually, sometimes, something that nobody thought could work that does work," adds Art Director John Mueller. "The Grotesque from *Diablo III* that explodes? Everybody remembers that monster."

BUCKLE

Environments

Players rarely see the sky in the *Diablo* universe except during cinematic interludes. While playing the games, players always look down. No glimpse of a horizon line ever promises passage to a better place, reinforcing the idea that the world of *Diablo* is harsh and bleak.

The downward-looking isometric view has been a defining characteristic of *Diablo* since the first release, which emphasized going down, down, down into the depths of the dungeon below the cathedral in Tristram.

Diablo II expanded Sanctuary with vast outdoor spaces, locations that bore names indicating diverse cultures, and dungeons designed with distinct aesthetics. "*Diablo II* opened up the game to all these different worlds," recalls Senior Art Director Samwise Didier. "It was the first time that you actually saw that there was a world, and a scary world, outside of that cathedral."

This expanded universe motivated the *Diablo III* art team to think about how each Act needed a different tonality to reinforce a sense of narrative progression, which they codified in a color script. Tonal variety manifested not only between areas but also within them, in order to provide "a little bit of surprise in the experience as you're progressing through the levels," explains Senior Art Supervisor Justin Thavirat. "So when you go into these dank, dark, desaturated catacombs, and you see the light of a candle in the corner, it's bright and warm—it's this little fresh breath of something."

This attention to detail opened up possibilities for environmental storytelling that allowed *Diablo III* artists to hint at the world's underpinning lore. The art team used "every opportunity to create a sense of history—that ancient, dark, decrepit, Gothic history—throughout the world," Thavirat says. "So things are destroyed, weathered, and worn down; cracked, overgrown, missing, broken. You always think about the environment as a main character."

Tristram

The Lord of Terror did not choose Tristram. His corrupting spirit was entombed there, deep beneath the dark woods, for centuries. But evil never rests, and the smallest whisper can tempt mortals to do almost anything.

Tristram has been a vital location in every *Diablo* game released thus far. The town's troubled and tragic history is written in the ruins of its manors, its restless graveyards, and its haunted survivors. This small town has been at the center of the darkest chapters in Sanctuary's history, and yet the people who live there stubbornly try to make peaceful lives for themselves, no matter how persistently the evil grows beneath their feet.

"Aboveground, normal people walk around, so we couldn't just riddle the environment with these awful things everywhere you turn," says Concept Artist Mark Gibbons. "There needed to be some sort of sense of an ecology."

Step outside the town walls, and countless horrors become apparent as the corrupting influence of hell reveals itself through the twisted landscape. The plant life has become poisonous and blood seeking, the tribes of unnerving goatmen have begun new hunts, and the spirits of the Fallen are lashing out.

"A lot of it just comes down to what you can do with a mixture of the natural habitat and the darkness that you introduce into the world," says Gibbons. "It's always fun to have the world be potentially threatening. You're never quite sure that you're safe just because you can't see an identifiable monster."

The Borderlands

nce Tyrael is restored at the end of *Diablo III*'s Act I, the heroes cross the sea and make their way to Caldeum. But before they can proceed to the great city and confront the dark power behind the Coven, they must first traverse the Borderlands, the barren wastes that surround the metropolis.

The *Diablo III* art team not only wanted the Borderlands to contrast with the desert surrounding Lut Gholein in *Diablo II*, but they also wanted to defy typical expectations of a desert as a barren wasteland with seemingly endless sand dunes, bright light, and a heat-hazed horizon.

Early concepts explored ideas such as envisioning the desert as an evaporated seabed, hinting at past civilizations through massive statuary buried in the sand, and making the desert a living place, nestling lush vegetation in chasms where it could grow in the deep shade, fostered by waterways constructed by the denizens who populate the land.

The artists finally settled on a combination of cracked, parched earth and jagged, clawlike dark rocks to define the Borderlands. "Ironically, a lot of the shapes for the rocks came from the rocks in Maui—where the lava hit the water and it made this swooshing kind of shape," says Concept Artist Trent Kaniuga.

Caldeum

A great trading center and crossroads, Caldeum is the capital of Kehjistan, standing in stark contrast to the corrupted ruins of Kurast in *Diablo II*. Known as the Jewel of the East, the city is ruled by the child emperor Hakan II, who surrounds himself with council members, merchants, and mages who jealously protect the power and wealth they have accumulated, making it the perfect place for Belial, the Lord of Lies, to amass influence in Sanctuary.

To design the capital city, the artists focused on creating contrast between the slums on the lower levels and the upper tiers, where the wealthy live. When designing the highest levels, Concept Artist Trent Kaniuga "wanted these walkways so you could look down and see the slums below. The wealthy people of Caldeum would have loved that—to look down upon the people who had less than them. There's a subliminal story that the player might realize if they're looking, but it's not explicitly told to you through any dialogue or quest."

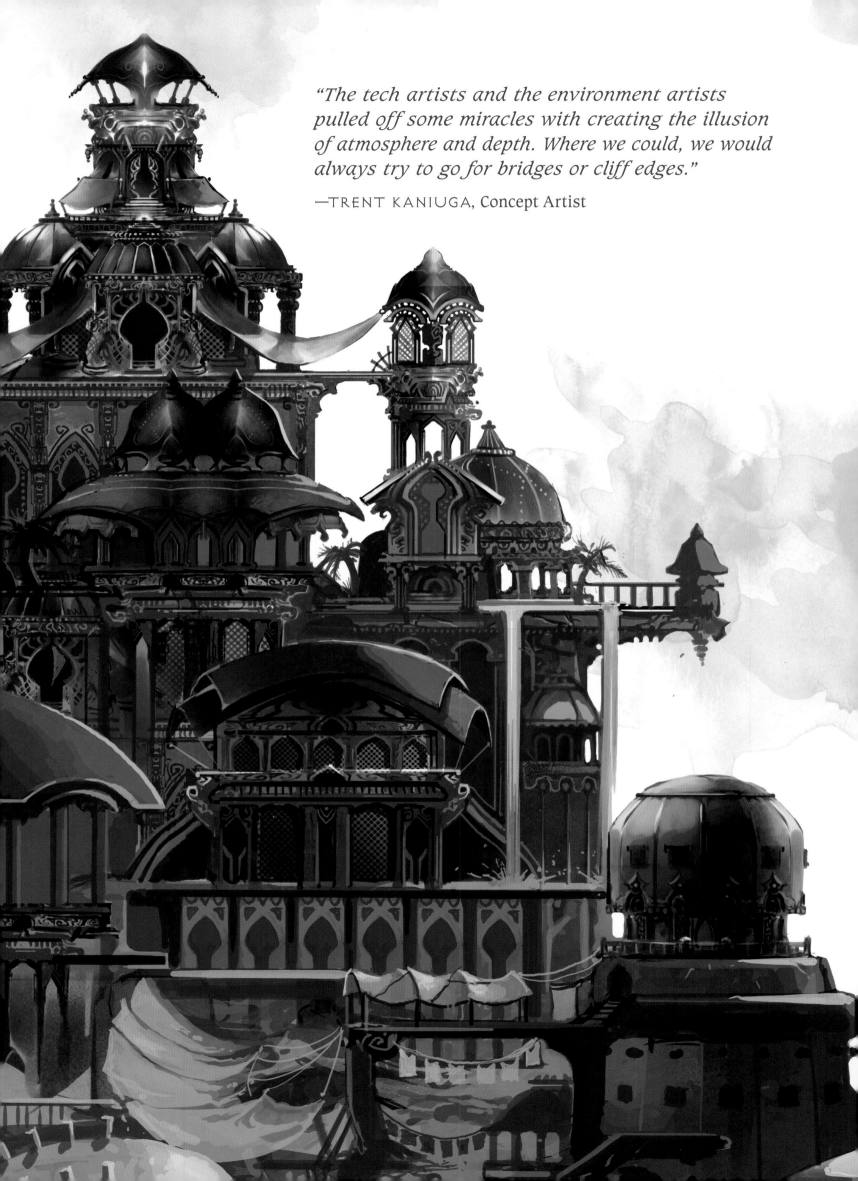

"*The tech artists and the environment artists pulled off some miracles with creating the illusion of atmosphere and depth. Where we could, we would always try to go for bridges or cliff edges.*"

—TRENT KANIUGA, Concept Artist

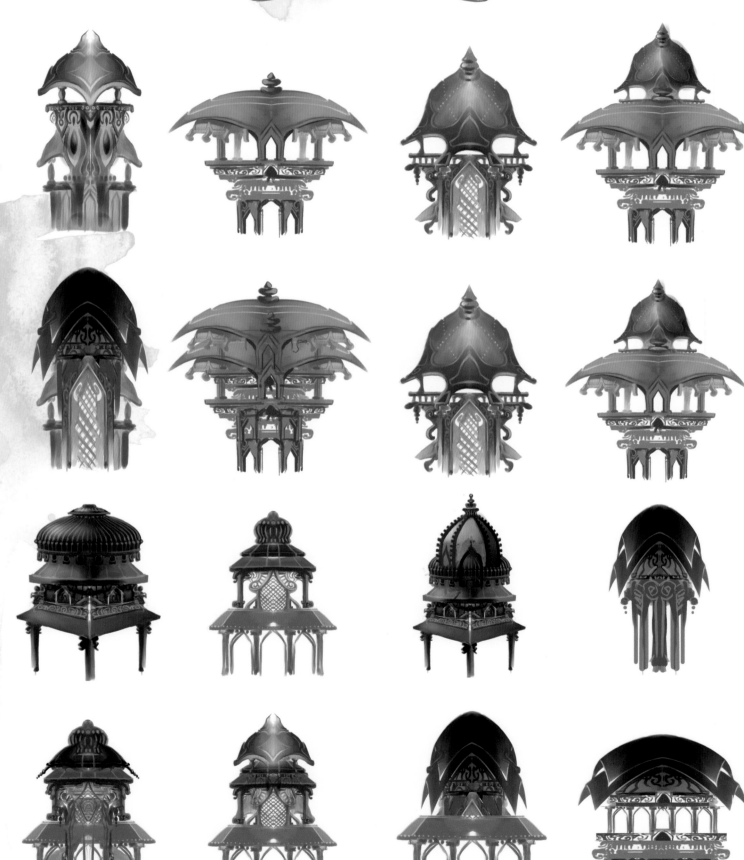

RIGHT Caldeum Slum House
Sketch + *Diablo III* + Sojin Hwang

BELOW RIGHT Caldeum Slum
Concept + *Diablo III* + Sojin Hwang

BOTTOM & OPPOSITE Caldeum Slum
Concepts + *Diablo III* + Peter Lee

Bastion's Keep

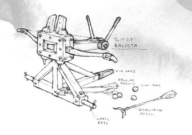

T he armies who once guarded Mount Arreat consider Bastion's Keep the site of their last stand against the demonic hordes that pour out of the Arreat Crater, where the mountain that housed the Worldstone used to be. A forgotten fortress, the keep has been fortified with makeshift timbers and found objects assembled with one goal in mind: defend it at all costs.

"The soldiers are like, 'This is our last holdout. We've got to push to defend this space. If we can defend this wall, then we can hold the demons back.' So they built all of these kind of shoddily constructed wooden structures," explains Concept Artist Trent Kaniuga. "That's why you've got all those cabers laid out, why you've got these different shape languages."

Full of neglected catapults, trebuchets, and other machines of war, the keep also houses a series of forges, which allowed the art team to bring hot reds and light-diffusing obscuring mist into the area, adding to the haunted, desperate sense of the place.

OPPOSITE Bastion's Keep Concept + *Diablo III* + Sojin Hwang

ABOVE Ballista Sketch + *Diablo III* + Victor Lee

BELOW Bastion Elements Sketches + *Diablo III* + Victor Lee

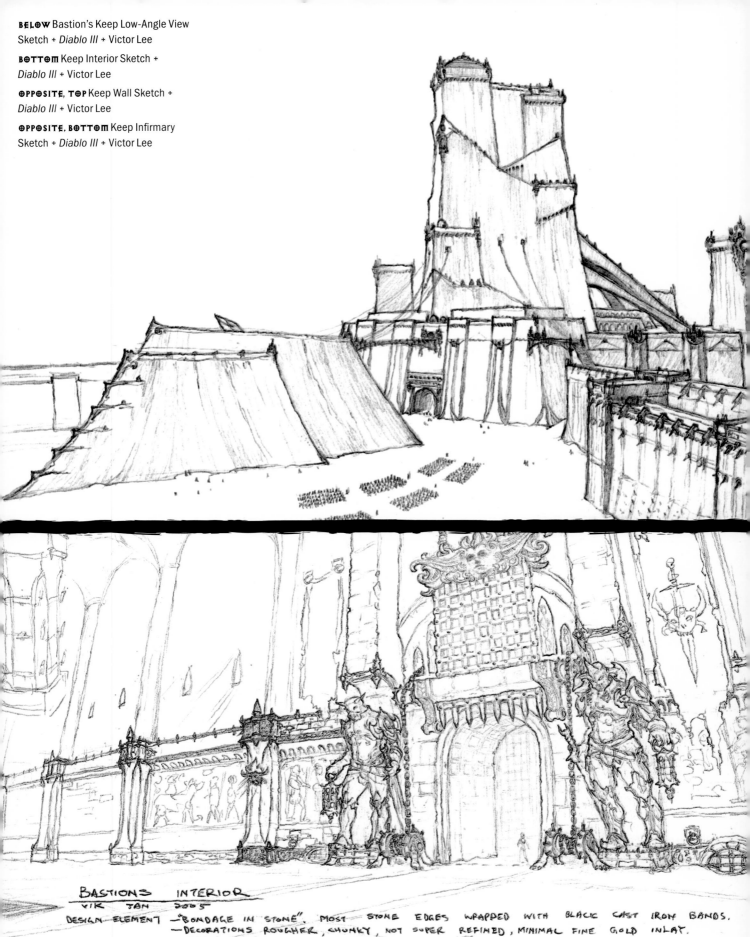

BELOW Bastion's Keep Low-Angle View
Sketch + *Diablo III* + Victor Lee

BOTTOM Keep Interior Sketch +
Diablo III + Victor Lee

OPPOSITE, TOP Keep Wall Sketch +
Diablo III + Victor Lee

OPPOSITE, BOTTOM Keep Infirmary
Sketch + *Diablo III* + Victor Lee

BASTIONS INTERIOR
VIK JAN 2005
DESIGN ELEMENT — "BONDAGE IN STONE". MOST STONE EDGES WRAPPED WITH BLACK CAST IRON BANDS.
— DECORATIONS ROUGHER, CHUNKY, NOT SUPER REFINED, MINIMAL FINE GOLD INLAY.
— GRAND, IMPOSING, LARGER THAN LIFE
MATERIAL — ROUGH CUT STONE, CAST IRON, STUDS, IRON RINGS.
SOME BRASS ? WOOD-DARK.
ATMOSHERE — FIRE LIT, MURKY, OCCASIONAL LIGHT SHAFTS.

LAYERED DEFENSIVE WALLS
VIK OCT 2004
- DARK STONE CONSTRUCTION
- CAST IRON SPIKS AND
  BANDING ON STONES.

FIRE SPOUT

BASTIONS KEEP INFIRMARY
VIK NOV 2004
- BLOOD DRENCHED CENTRAL AMPUTATION STATION
- BODIES AND PARTS DISPOSED OF IN CENTRAL PIT.
- GRATING SERVES AS EFFICIENT DRAIN FOR BLOOD.
- LIGHT RAYS FROM HIGH WINDOWS PENETRATE GLOOM.
- AREA LITTERED WITH DISCARDED WEAPONS, SHIELDS AND
  ARMOR PIECES, AS WELL AS PRIMITIVE SURGICAL
  INSTRUMENTS, SAWS, CLAMPS .....
- SHOULD FEEL ANCIENT, DARK, DANK, USED, WET, LIKE ABATTOIR

Arreat

For thousands of years, the barbarian tribes protected Mount Arreat and the secret held within it, repelling anyone who tried to draw upon the power of the Worldstone, the ancient instrument that created Sanctuary and hid the realm from the Eternal Conflict.

But even the mightiest barbarians could not stand against Baal's tide of destruction. It fell to Tyrael, the angelic Aspect of Justice, to destroy the Worldstone before Baal could corrupt it, unleashing a cataclysm upon the region and turning the area into a smoking crater.

When developing what Arreat Crater would look like in *Diablo III*—and who would inhabit it—the *Diablo* art team tried to imagine what all the destructive horror Baal had imbued into the Worldstone could give rise to. "It was almost natural that the crater was made out of bones and skins," says Concept Artist Sojin Hwang. "I started developing an idea that when this dark energy erupted, it claimed almost everything in the area, such as houses, buildings, and any living creatures around it, violently swallowing its surroundings. Therefore, you can see sharp spikes along the cliffside, along with stretched, skin-like surface textures and a variety of bone elements."

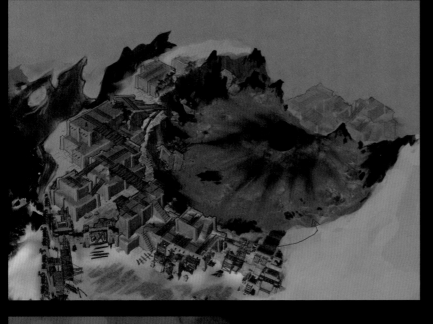

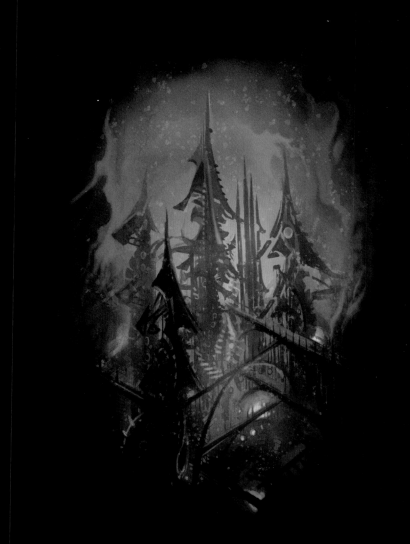

ABOVE, RIGHT & BELOW Arreat
Sketches + *Diablo III* + Trent Kaniuga
OPPOSITE Crater Tower Concept +
Diablo III + Victor Lee

The High Heavens

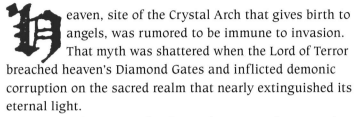

ABOVE & BELOW Judgment Chamber Ceiling Sketches + *Diablo III* + Chris Thunig

RIGHT Judgment Chamber Entrance Sketch + *Diablo III* + Chris Thunig

BOTTOM Gates of Heaven Concept + *Diablo III* + Trent Kaniuga

OPPOSITE Heaven Concept + *Diablo III* + Peter Lee

Heaven, site of the Crystal Arch that gives birth to angels, was rumored to be immune to invasion. That myth was shattered when the Lord of Terror breached heaven's Diamond Gates and inflicted demonic corruption on the sacred realm that nearly extinguished its eternal light.

Visual concepts for the High Heavens began with attempts to picture the iconic gates. Initial ideas for them envision much wider and imposing structures than the final almost-delicate depictions. But the first concepts firmly established the importance of a circular shape at the center. "Early on, we got that idea of the thin, ornate pattern work with the circular elements everywhere," recalls Concept Artist Trent Kaniuga. "It went through a lot of modification after that."

Eventually, the central round shape was incorporated into the Silver Spire, which came to be emblematic of the ultimate design direction for the High Heavens. "Our goal was to symbolize the identity and design language for the High Heavens in this one concept image, to establish a visual direction," says Concept Artist Sojin Hwang. "We really wanted to communicate the sense of light and its power."

Against the light, there is always the dark, of course. "For heaven, I tried to convey a feeling of purity—like gold, white marble, things like that," muses Lead Concept Artist Victor Lee. "So that when we design a hellish demonic place, we have the whole range to play with. We can go dark. We can go bloody. We can give maximum range to the artists."

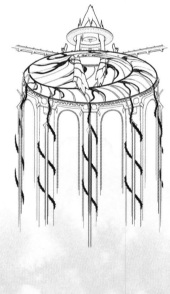

"*Our camera is fixed, so a lot of the time, the only place I could go is down, because we can never see the sky. You go deeper and deeper. In heaven, you can see all the way down. If I can only look down, then I want to look down all the way.*"

—VICTOR LEE, Lead Concept Artist

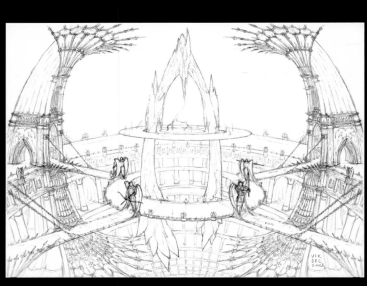

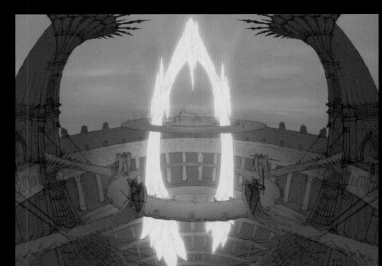

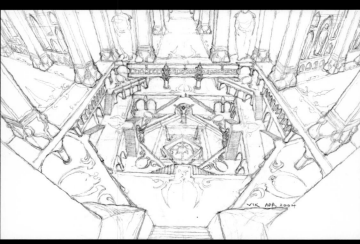

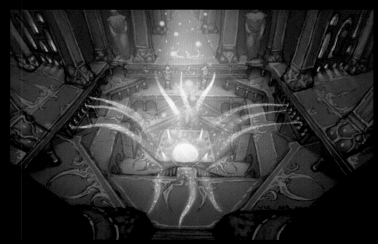

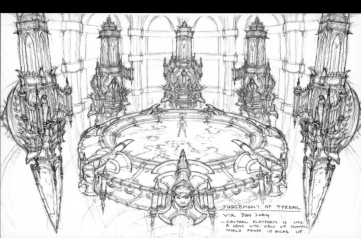

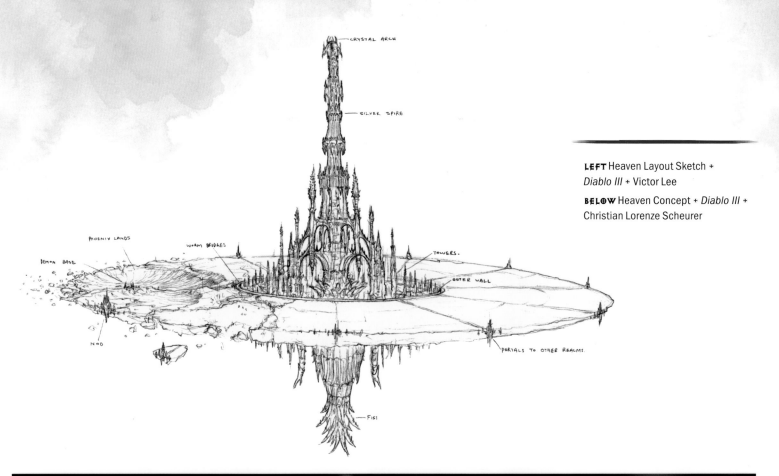

CRYSTAL ARCH

SILVER SPIRE

PHOENIX LANDS

WORM BRIDGES

DEMON BASE

TOWERS.

OUTER WALL

NOD

PORTALS TO OTHER REALMS.

FIST

LEFT Heaven Layout Sketch + *Diablo III* + Victor Lee

BELOW Heaven Concept + *Diablo III* + Christian Lorenze Scheurer

VIK   JJUN 2004

INTERIOR
SILVER SPIRE

OPPOSITE Silver Spire Interior Concept + *Diablo III* + Victor Lee

FAR LEFT Silver Spire Concept + *Diablo III* + Sojin Hwang

LEFT & BELOW Silver Spire Exterior Studies + *Diablo III* + Sojin Hwang

BOTTOM Silver Spire Interior Study + *Diablo III* + Sojin Hwang

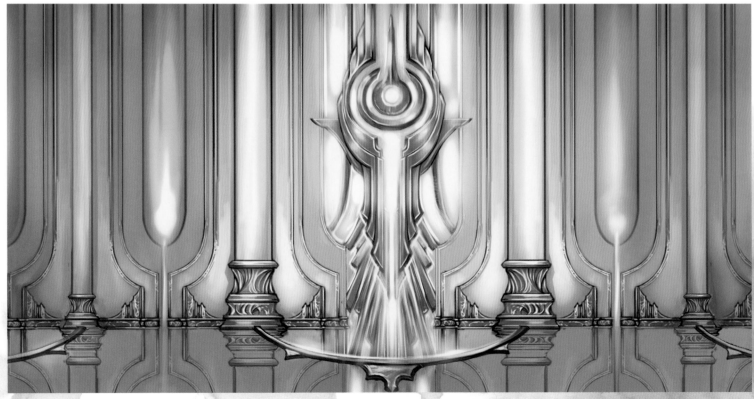

Westmarch

nce a bustling center of trade that was the greatest city in Sanctuary, according to Deckard Cain, Westmarch was built by the conqueror Rakkis, with thick walls so that it could withstand any siege. Nevertheless, the metropolis easily fell to Malthael and his army of Reapers, turning many of the city's defenders into disturbing undead and setting the stage for *Diablo III*'s *Reaper of Souls* expansion.

The environmental design for Westmarch had to convey its impressive size, reflect its rich but troubled history, and feature its defining architectural element—the massive stone walls meant to repel invaders. Working closely with the 3-D environment artists to create assets that could be stacked together in different configurations, Concept Artist Sojin Hwang was able to develop a consistent look for the city while supporting a modular approach to engineering its imposing sense of scale. "I would design different building types and shapes and then dismantle them into pieces so we could easily reassemble them into different buildings and assets," she says.

Recombined like the parts of the Frankenstein monster, these city elements paint a picture of a haunted place where evil lurks in the shadows. "*Reaper of Souls*: that was when the game pivoted back toward the dark feel of *Diablo II*," comments Art Director John Mueller. "Westmarch and *Reaper of Souls* felt very grounded—and a lot more based in a world than a fantastical place."

OPPOSITE Westmarch Concept + *Diablo III: Reaper of Souls* + Sojin Hwang

ABOVE Westmarch Building "E" Sketch + *Diablo III: Reaper of Souls* + Sojin Hwang

BELOW Westmarch Sketch + *Diablo III: Reaper of Souls* + Sojin Hwang

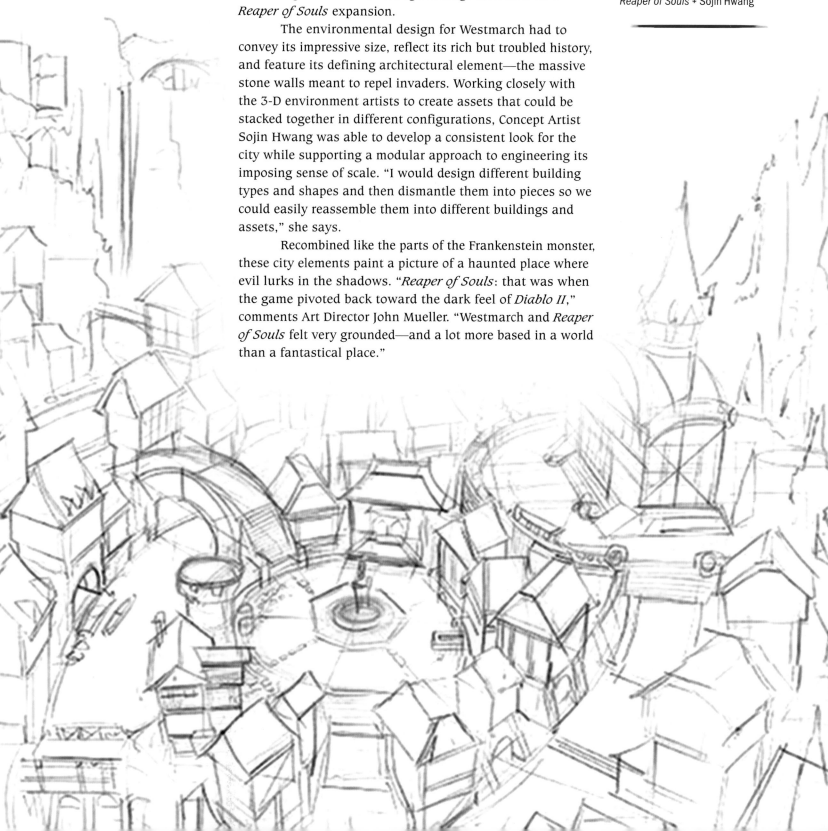

ABOVE Base Building Variation "A" Sketches + *Diablo III: Reaper of Souls* + Sojin Hwang

RIGHT Add-ons for Building Variation "A" Sketches + *Diablo III: Reaper of Souls* + Sojin Hwang

BELOW Iterations of Building Variation "A" + *Diablo III: Reaper of Souls* + Sojin Hwang

Pandemonium

228

ABOVE Pandemonium Sketch + *Diablo III: Reaper of Souls* + Victor Lee

BOTTOM LEFT Portal Guardian Sketch + *Diablo III: Reaper of Souls* + Victor Lee

BOTTOM RIGHT Pandemonium Sketch + *Diablo III: Reaper of Souls* + Grace Liu

OPPOSITE Pandemonium Concept + *Diablo III: Reaper of Souls* + Peter Lee

Pandemonium is the name given to the scar torn in the fabric of the universe by the battles between Anu and Tathamet, which gave rise to heaven, hell, angels, and demons. A place that stands to the side of established existence, Pandemonium is a primal realm that is in a state of constant change.

"Pandemonium is a really abstract place," says Lead Concept Artist Victor Lee. "I can't really nail down physically where it is. It's not heaven, and it's not hell. We had to come up with a design that communicates that. One version of Pandemonium is basically a spinning disk almost like the Milky Way. It's rotating slowly. And as this world rotates, the edges break off and form their own little islands. It's a constantly changing landscape—a chunk of land that is almost alive."

RIGHT Pandemonium Landscape Study + *Diablo III: Reaper of Souls* + Victor Lee

BELOW Pandemonium Concept + *Diablo III: Reaper of Souls* + Victor Lee

OPPOSITE, TOP Pandemonium Mood Study + *Diablo III: Reaper of Souls* + Josh Tallman

A Return to Darkness

From the early days of Diablo IV's development, the goal was to embrace the sinister side of Sanctuary and bring the darkness of the series to the fore once again.

"I think Diablo IV will carve out a fresh way of seeing the world while returning the visuals to Diablo's dark, Gothic, medieval roots," says Diablo IV Art Director John Mueller.

Diablo IV's artistic vision was built using several key pillars: "Return to Darkness," "Embrace the Legacy," and what the art team calls the "Old Masters Pillar," which is shorthand for striving to make each part of the new game look like it was painted by a venerated artist such as Rembrandt or Ilya Repin. When researching lighting or surface, they looked at old paintings first, rather than contemporary video games, with the aim of interpreting the world of *Diablo* like a medieval painter might versus how a photographer would.

"When you're on the surface of the world of Sanctuary, things feel very grounded in the medieval world," says Mueller. "But as soon as you go into a dungeon or a cave, that's when things get really dark and evil."

To return to darkness, the art team, comprising veterans from *Diablo II* and *Diablo III*, drew on its memories of past releases' examples of strong Gothic aesthetics and grim, unforgiving, gritty fantasy. Excited to merge aspects they love from all games in the franchise under this unifying vision, they tended to favor darker, more sophisticated color palettes.

"There're a lot of things that we want to honor—dungeons were such a great experience in *Diablo III*," says Mueller. "And then there's the tone of the world from *Diablo II* and the desperate sense of the world in *Diablo*. The team is so excited to reach into those dark corners of our imaginations and bring that world to our fans."

like our own medieval era. We developed the idea that the masterful artists of Sanctuary would immortalize events that happened thousands of years ago through their art."

—JOHN MUELLER, Art Director

RIGHT Pentagram Sketch +
Diablo IV + Richie Marella

BELOW Lilith Concept +
Diablo IV + Josh Tallman

BOTTOM Lilith Concept +
Diablo IV + Victor Lee

OPPOSITE Lilith + *Diablo IV* + Brom

RIGHT Drowned Concept +
Diablo IV + Ryan Metcalf

BELOW Drowned Family Concepts +
Diablo IV + Victor Lee

OPPOSITE Drowned Raider Concepts +
Diablo IV + Mike Franchina

242

THESE PAGES Goatmen Key Art + *Diablo IV* + Igor Sidorenko

THESE PAGES Cultist Concepts +
Diablo IV + Ted Beargeon

ACKNOWLEDGMENTS

Over the past three decades, hundreds of committed artists, designers, and developers have shaped the unique experience that is *Diablo*, inspiring legions of fans to embrace the darkness while relentlessly battling to keep it from consuming the world of Sanctuary. Thank you all, inspired creators, for your vision, tireless efforts, and commitment to making the best games possible. Your indispensable contributions have helped establish a great tradition.

Thank you, too, to everyone at Blizzard and Blizzard North who had a hand in bringing these amazing games to the world. Without your hard work and support, *Diablo* might never have found its passionate audience.

Most importantly, thank you to the millions of committed players who have explored Sanctuary and made it their own. Stay awhile longer and listen. There are still more stories to tell.

COLOPHON

WRITTEN & EDITED BY Jake Gerli
ADDITIONAL WRITING Robert Brooks
CREATIVE CONSULTATION Luis Barriga, John Mueller, Sebastian Stepien
LORE CONSULTATION Sean Copeland, Christi Kugler, Justin Parker
PRODUCTION Brianne M. Loftis, Timothy Loughran, Paul Morrissey, Alix Nicholaeff, Derek Rosenberg, Cara Samuelsen
DIRECTOR, CONSUMER PRODUCTS Byron Parnell
DIRECTORS, CREATIVE DEVELOPMENT Ralph Sanchez and David Seeholzer
SPECIAL THANKS Brom, Jeff Chamberlain, Paul David, Samwise Didier, Chris Donelson, Aaron Gaines, Phroilan Gardner, Mark Gibbons, Sojin Hwang, Jeramiah Johnson, Trent Kaniuga, Victor Lee, Timothy Linn, Josh Manning, Richie Marella, James McCoy, Chris Metzen, John Mueller, John Polidora, Matthew Ryan, Josh Tallman, Justin Thavirat, Chris Thunig, Paul Warzecha, Kenson Yu

DESIGNED BY Cameron + Companyr
PUBLISHER Chris Gruener
CREATIVE DIRECTOR Iain R. Morris
DESIGNER Robert Dolgaard
MANAGING EDITOR Jan Hughes

Published by Blizzard Entertainment
Irvine, California, in 2019. No part of this book may be reproduced in any form without permission from the publisher.

Library of Congress Cataloging-in-Publication Data available.

Trade ISBN: 978-1-945683-65-7
Collector's Edition ISBN: 978-1-950366-09-5

Manufactured in China

Print run 10 9 8 7 6 5 4 3 2 1

FRONT COVER Diablo + *Diablo III* + Brom **BACK COVER** Tyrael + *Diablo III* + Brom **PAGE 1** Diablo + *Diablo III* + Brom **PAGES 2–3** Key Art + *Diablo* Twentieth Anniversary + Alex Horley **PAGE 4** The Butcher + *Diablo III* + Brom **PAGE 5** Fig. VIII Sigil + *Book of Adria: A Diablo Bestiary* + Fernando Forero **PAGE 6** Diablo Versus Imperius + *Diablo III* + Alex Horley **PAGE 7** Symbol of the Order of the Hordadrim + *Diablo* Game Manual + Samwise Didier **PAGES 252–253** Andariel Key Art + *Diablo IV* + Victor Lee **PAGES 254–255** Hell Gate Key Art + *Diablo IV* + Igor Sidorenko **ABOVE** Ashava Concept + *Diablo IV* + Victor Lee